CHOPPERS

CHOPPERS

THUNDER IN THE SKY

ROBERT GENAT

MetroBooks

MetroBooks

An Imprint of Friedman/Fairfax Publishers

© 1998 by Michael Friedman Publishing Group, Inc.

Library of Congress Cataloging-in-Publication data available upon request.

ISBN 1-56799-615-9

Editor: Nathaniel Marunas
Art Director: Kevin Ullrich
Designer: Jonathan Gaines
Photography Editor: Wendy Missan
Production Manager: Jeanne E. Hutter

Printed in China by Leefung-Asco Printers Ltd

10 9 8 7 6 5 4 3 2 1

For bulk purchases and special sales, please contact:
Friedman/Fairfax Publishers
Attention: Sales Department
15 West 26th Street
New York, NY 10010
212/685-6610 FAX 212/685-1307

Visit our website:
http://www.metrobooks.com

Acknowledgments

As with any project of this scope, there are many people who participate in various ways. Some folks provide important hard data and others show you the way to otherwise unlikely sources of key information. Some people are nice enough to share their experiences flying in helicopters and others offer you a chance to ride along with them.

Thanks to the U.S. Navy's LTJG Charlie Brown, AIRPAC Public Affairs Office; LCDR Scott Harris, Public Affairs Officer USS *Abraham Lincoln*; and helicopter pilot LCDR Jeff Hogan. Thanks to the following United States Coast Guard pilots for their cooperation: LT Lisa Blow, LT Tim Tobiasz, and CDR John Long. Thanks to the San Diego Police Department's Air Support Unit pilots Sgt. Pete Munholand, Officer Teresa Clark, and Officer Kevin Means. Thanks to the U.S. Army Helicopter Museum and U.S. Army pilot LTC Rick Rife.

A special thanks to the following people for their help: Hal Klopper from McDonnell Douglas; Joe Kaggis from Boeing Sikorsky; William Yarber from Bell Helicopter Textron; Jonathan Arms from Arms Communications; and my good friend and co-conspirator, Hans Halberstadt from Very Moving Pictures.

Dedication

To my mother and father, Frances and Oscar Genat. Thanks for your unconditional love and for the many important lessons you taught me.

CONTENTS

TITLE PAGE: The newest helicopter in the U.S. Coast Guard's
inventory is the HH-60J
Jayhawk. The Jayhawk carries a
four-man crew and is capable of
landing on the decks of
Hamilton- and *Bear-*class Coast
Guard cutters.

HALF-TITLE PAGE: The SH-3 Sea
King has been a mainstay of the
U.S. Navy's helicopter force for
more than twenty years. During
Desert Shield/Desert Storm, carrier-based Sea Kings logged
more than five thousand hours
conducting combat search-and-
rescue, logistics support, and
mine-locating missions.

CONTENTS PAGE: Armed to the
teeth with four Hellfire missiles
(inboard station) and a missile
launcher with nineteen missiles
under each wing, this U.S. Army
AH-64 Apache is ready for
action.

INTRODUCTION

The unique sound of helicopter rotor blades biting into the air is as common today as the sound of any of humankind's mechanical inventions on which we have come to rely. Helicopters have become part of our everyday lives. Television news, sports coverage, tourism, law enforcement, medicine, agriculture, and the military have all felt the impact of the helicopter.

The earliest visions of flight were of vertical flight. Long before the Wright brothers launched from Kitty Hawk, avia-tion enthusiasts were trying to figure out how a machine might rise vertically into the sky. Several early pioneers made it possible, risking their lives and spending their fortunes in the process. Our debt to these early dreamers is great.

The advent of war, however, was to be the environment in which the helicopter and its development would flourish. The success of the Bell 47 signaled the future of the helicopter and its importance to the military effort. The role of the Bell 47 as the first air ambulance for soldiers wounded on the bat-tlefields of Korea brought immediate acceptance to this rela-tively new flying machine.

Next, the introduction of the turboshaft engine gave the helicopter more power to fly farther and carry heavier loads. The war in the jungles of Vietnam pushed the helicopter into the national forefront. Troops were delivered by helicopter to the battle zone and were later rescued by helicopter from unimaginable horrors. The helicopter permitted unconven-tional warfare in an unconventional war.

A natural evolution of the rescue helicopter into an offensive weapon took place out of a need to protect not only the troops on the ground but the helicopter crews and their human cargo. The Huey Cobra became the first military heli-copter designed specifically for an offensive role. Helicopter manufacturers responded quickly with new helicopters for specialized missions. The success of the Huey Cobra led to the development of the deadly Apache—the tank killer. Cockpit technology once reserved for jet fighters became standard in the modern attack helicopter.

Municipalities now routinely purchase helicopters for law enforcement and emergency medical service (EMS) missions. Forward-looking infrared (FLIR) imagers first used in combat are now commonplace on most urban police helicopters.

Large, well-funded counties deploy multiple EMS heli-copters, fully equipped with state-of-the-art medical equip-ment to improve survival rates for patients en route to hospi-tals. Law enforcement agencies with large geographical juris-dictions over rugged terrain have search-and-rescue heli-copters. Helicopters routinely rescue fallen hikers, boaters, and drivers who think they can make it across just one more flood-ed road.

In the tourism industry, helicopters fly over scenic land-scapes as a form of entertainment and education. Helicopters transport skiers to mountaintops covered in virgin snowfall. Helicopters transport rafters out of the Grand Canyon after weeklong trips down the Colorado River.

Other fields where the helicopter is indispensable include television news, sports coverage, agriculture, animal rescue and species preservation, cattle ranching, geology, and VIP air-taxi service.

Some simple guidelines were used to select the heli-copters featured in this book. Helicopters deemed historically meaningful are covered, such as the Russian Ka-50 Hokum, the first helicopter with an ejection seat. Also featured are heli-copters that represent the best examples of their type—such as the world's largest heavy-duty transport helicopter, the Russian Mi-26 Halo—or of design, such as the agile attack helicopter known as the AH-64 Apache. It was important also to include helicopters that have enjoyed a long service career and those adaptable to a variety of roles, like the Bell 47 and the Huey. Finally, helicopters were chosen that represent a significant technological advance, like the RAH-66 Comanche, with its stealthy fuselage design.

The United States and Russia have long been and remain the leaders in technology and innovation, and most of the helicopters featured in this book are either U.S. or Russian mil-itary models. Both countries are and have been prolific manu-facturers of rotary wing aircraft, their technology long driven by military necessity. Both developed and built highly specialized machines to meet specific battlefield needs. Although other countries have produced helicopters, these were, for the most part, largely based on designs already in circulation.

Advancements in military helicopter design found their way into the civilian market. The company that built the rugged Bell 47 and the Huey for military use went on to build the versatile Bell JetRanger, one of the most popular light-turbine helicopters in civilian use today. Today, lighter fuselages, stronger mechanical components, more powerful and reliable engines, and better control mechanisms make the helicopter a dependable civilian tool.

If only the early pioneers had lived to see what their great flopping, bouncing, and whirring machines would become.

The MD 600N is the newest NOTAR (for "no tail rotor") helicopter from McDonnell Douglas. It's a stretched-out version of the original NOTAR, the MD 520N. The longer fuselage on the 600N provides enough room to seat eight. Arizona's AirStar Helicopter uses this 600N for tours over the Grand Canyon. The 600N's quiet NOTAR technology addresses the problem of flying over an area sensitive to noise pollution.

CHAPTER

1

A SHORT HISTORY OF HELICOPTER DEVELOPMENT

The development of the modern helicopter can be divided into three phases. During the first phase, early enthusiasts dabbled with model-size prototypes and ran headlong into the seemingly insurmountable obstacles of lift, torque, and control. What emerged from this period was an unrelenting fascination with the notion of vertical flight. The second phase was characterized by ideas founded in science and in the laws of aerodynamics. A significant breakthrough in the 1920s led to a third phase, characterized by better design, performance, and application. By the early 1930s, engineers had finally conquered the problems of weight, torque, lift, and control. Ongoing advancements in design would continue to perfect the helicopter into what we know today as a reliable and versatile tool of everyday life.

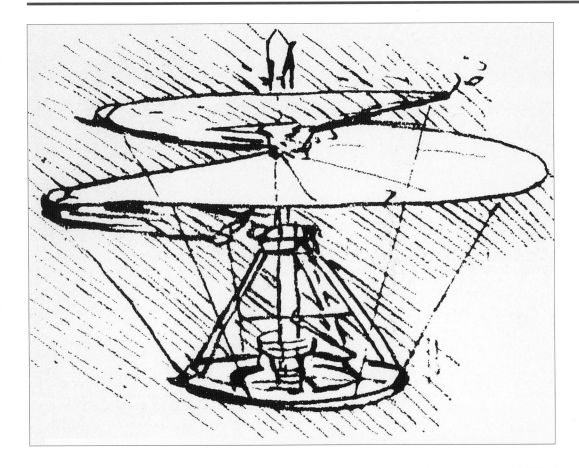

PREVIOUS PAGE: This experimental helicopter design illustrates the lengths to which early aeronautical engineers went to conquer the obstacles to vertical flight. How will these wings operate to keep the craft aloft? What is the power source? Once off the ground, how will the direction, speed, and altitude be controlled? These men are pondering these questions, and others, including who will be the pilot?

ABOVE: This 1483 sketch by Leonardo da Vinci (1452–1519) is one of the first documented designs of a device that might fly under its own power. Da Vinci's drawings inspired many inventors and scientists, including a young Igor Sikorsky, who made his first helicopter model at age twelve.

E E (1768 1880)

The first phase of helicopter development began with humankind's fascination with the notion of vertical flight. This idea had been inspired by an ancient Chinese flying toy and by the sketches of Leonardo da Vinci. During this period, from the mid-1700s to the early 1880s, enthusiasts experimented with model-size prototypes. Their work served to maintain an interest in the quest for vertical flight and to identify the specific questions yet to be answered, namely, what is the best power source, how can torque be eliminated, and how can this unwieldy craft be controlled for safe and sustained flight?

Numerous fanciful theories were tossed out as answers to these questions. In 1768, a French mathematician named J.P. Paucton thought that an old method of lifting water, the Archimedean screw, could be applied to solve the problem of vertical flight. In 1784, two Frenchmen, Messrs. Launoy and Bienvenu, experimented with a bowspring as a power source

for a small model they had designed. They also introduced the concept of counter-rotating propellers. Each turning propeller offset the thrust of the other, thereby eliminating torque, the turning and twisting force that results from a single rotating propeller. With their small model, the two Frenchmen had demonstrated the use of a power source (the bowspring) and a method to minimize torque (counter-rotating propellers).

Early enthusiasts experimented with a variety of power sources. Englishman W.H. Phillips demonstrated in 1842 a model helicopter powered by steam. Too heavy to fly, it was unsuccessful, and Phillips gave up. Viscount Gustave de Ponton d'Amecourt of France experimented with models powered by steam and by a clockwork mechanism. The power was never sufficient to lift its own weight. D'Amecourt called his models *hélicoptères*, from the Greek words for "spiral" (*heliko*) and "wing" (*pteron*). Thomas Edison experimented with batteries as a power source, but they were much too heavy for the craft, which could lift only a few pounds. Although he abandoned his helicopter research, Edison believed strongly that ongoing experimentation by engineers would one day result in a successful design.

S S (1900 1920)

The second phase of development was characterized by the work of engineers and scientists who better understood the laws of physics and aerodynamics and who benefited from the discoveries coming out of the advancements in fixed-wing flight.

Frenchman Louis-Charles Breguet, an engineer and aviation enthusiast, was determined to design an aircraft capable of vertical flight. News in 1903 of the Wright brothers' first flight fueled his passion.

Using a 40-horsepower Antoinette engine as a power source, Breguet and a team of engineers and benefactors created a ridiculous-looking craft that nonetheless lifted itself and a hapless pilot off the ground. The craft hovered at an altitude of two feet (61cm) for one minute. Ground crew stationed around the Breguet-Richet Gyroplane No. 1 held the corners

TOP: Frenchman Paul Cornu experimented with various designs, including the one pictured here. On November 13, 1907, Cornu's 573-pound (260kg) craft, powered by a 24-horsepower engine, was able to hover one foot (30cm) off the ground for several minutes.

BOTTOM: Spanish engineer Juan de la Cierva built his first autogiro in 1926, introducing the concept of autorotation. The fuselage was that of a conventional fixed-wing aircraft, minus the wings. The nose-mounted piston engine drove the craft forward into the airstream, and the rotating blades lifted it off the ground. Ten years later, the Autogiro Company of America would be demonstrating the Pitcairn AC-35, an autogiro designed to be driven on the road once it landed. The rotor blades could be folded back over the fuselage and the propeller disengaged for ground travel.

what might happen. A young Igor Sikorsky worked unsuccessfully to overcome the problems of lift, vibration, and control. He suspended his efforts on the helicopter in 1910, devoting himself to the design and production of fixed-wing aircraft. He would later return to his first love, the helicopter.

Other engineers who attempted vertical flight included Jacob C.H. Ellehammer of Denmark; Emile Berliner, a German immigrant to the United States; George de Bothezat, a Russian refugee, also to the United States; and French engineer Étienne Oehmichen. Raul Pateras Pescara of Spain came up with what seemed to be a step forward. He designed a helicopter with two rotors that spun in opposite directions, but the craft could not be controlled. Despite these efforts, the evolution of the helicopter sputtered to a halt. No one seemed able to offer a workable design. Everyone was waiting for a breakthrough.

AUTOROTATION AND FLAPPING HINGES

The breakthrough phase began in the early 1920s, with the work of Spaniard Juan de la Cierva. He was the first engineer to "crack the code" in deciphering the central stumbling blocks to controlled, sustained rotary-wing flight. The first thing he figured out was that the principles of lift and flight attributed to a fixed wing would also apply to a rotary wing. As long as the wing was moving through an airstream, lift would occur. In Cierva's early tests, a conventional engine-driven nose propeller moved the aircraft forward. Meanwhile, rotors positioned on top of the fuselage would begin to rotate, creating lift as they traveled through the airstream. This was known as autorotation. This new aircraft was called an autogiro. Since the rotor blades on top of the fuselage were not power-driven, the phenomenon of torque did not occur. An autogiro is unable to hover or jump start into vertical flight, but the understanding of autorotation pointed engineers in the right direction toward future developments.

Cierva discovered, however, that another problem emerged—the inequality of lift. As the rotors moved, the advancing blade (wing) would pick up airspeed while the retreating blade would lose airspeed. In 1922, Cierva came up

to prevent it from tipping over. Breguet continued his research and experimental helicopter flights until 1909, when he decided to devote himself entirely to the manufacture of fixed-wing airplanes.

Other engineers were meanwhile working on their own helicopter designs. French engineer Paul Cornu designed a much lighter model and had several successful ascents; but the problem of control remained. Once aloft, there was no telling with the notion of flapping hinges. With this innovation, each blade was hinged in a horizontal plane at the point where it joined the hub, allowing the blade to move (flap) up or down. The advancing blade would lift up (decreasing its angle of attack) and the retreating blade would flap down (increasing its angle of attack), thereby equalizing lift among the rotating blades. This is considered Cierva's significant contribution to rotary-wing flight.

Cierva continued to experiment. His achievements were significant enough to merit a contract from the British government in 1925. He established his own company in England in 1926 and soon could not keep pace with the demand for his autogiro. In the late 1920s, he began granting production licenses to foreign manufacturers.

One of these licenses was sold to U.S. aircraft builder Harold Pitcairn, who made his first autogiro flight in America in 1928. Pitcairn continued to experiment with Cierva's autogiro design. In 1932, Pitcairn pitched the autogiro to the American public in a glossy advertising campaign intended to appeal to those wealthy individuals left standing after the stock market crash of 1929. His colorful ads depicted the still well-to-do flying onto the grounds of their country clubs or landing in isolated hunting camps for a weekend of sport. Although Pitcairn's ads and the autogiro intrigued the American public and became an object of considerable fascination, the craft did not become the commercial success he had envisioned. Pitcairn stopped promoting the vehicle to the general public in 1933.

Despite the lack of significant sales in the civilian market, the autogiro was used by American industry and business in various ways during the early 1930s. The New Jersey State Forest Service used it for fire fighting; businesses used the autogiro to tow banners promoting their products; and a few newspapers used the autogiro to cover breaking stories. It was also employed for crop dusting, archaeological surveys, and short-run mail deliveries. A ceremony on the White House lawn in 1931 honored Harold Pitcairn for bringing the autogiro to the United States.

The next milestone in helicopter development also came from Juan de la Cierva. In 1933, his work culminated in what we recognize today as the "jump start." He designed a system that allowed the pilot to control the pitch of the rotor blades, which were now powered by a gear and clutch mechanism instead of the old method of autorotation. The blades would spin flat, gaining speed, but no lift would occur. As soon as the mechanism was declutched, the blades would bite into the air and cause the aircraft to jump vertically. These early experiments with collective pitch control would ultimately lead to a design that would allow the rotor itself to be tilted.

Juan de la Cierva died in 1936 as a passenger on a Dutch commercial airliner that crashed in foggy weather as it took off from London's Croydon Aerodrome. With his death, interest

OPPOSITE: Like many early aviation enthusiasts, Frenchman Louis Charles Breguet (1880–1955) devoted his energies to fixed-wing flight as well as to vertical flight. He began building airplanes in 1905. The planes were used in World War I. One made the first Paris–New York flight shortly after Lindbergh's historic flight in 1927.

LEFT: Juan de la Cierva poses upon his arrival in New York aboard the passenger liner *Bremen,* on November 11, 1930. De la Cierva was responsible not only for discovering the phenomenon of autorotation but also for making the significant advances in rotor technology that eventually made possible what we now know as the "jump start" (vertical takeoff) and the process of collective pitch control.

British autogiro pilots Amberse Banks, C.J. Faulkner, and Arthur Rawson were the first to fly an autogiro in the United States. After a thirty-minute demonstration flight on December 21, 1928, they landed at Pitcairn Field in Philadelphia.

in the autogiro began to wane in the United States. Autogiro manufacturers were struggling to make a profit: the military was not interested in an autogiro with limited speed, range, and cargo-carrying capacity; and private and commercial interest was fading in favor of the less costly, more dependable fixed-wing aircraft.

ADVANCEMENTS IN DESIGN, PERFORMANCE, AND APPLICATION (1937 TO 1944)

The next step forward was made by German pilot and aircraft manufacturer Henrich Focke. After purchasing a license to build autogiros, he began testing his theories of vertical flight. His goal was to design a true helicopter, one in which the rotor blades had their own power source. In the spring of 1937, his Fa-61 shattered every official helicopter record to date. The Focke Fa-61 climbed to an altitude of 7,800 feet (2,377.4m). Focke also demonstrated that in the event of an engine failure, this helicopter could make a safe, autorotational landing.

The German government awarded Henrich Focke a contract to produce a larger version of the Fa-61, one that could

Designed by German engineer Henrich Focke, this experimental helicopter, with two triple-bladed rotors, captured the attention of an American engineer who took the picture in late 1938 during a visit abroad. This is possibly the forerunner of what would later be known as the "Drache," a twin-rotor design heavily funded by the German government.

RIGHT: Anton Flettner (1885–1961) in London at age thirty-nine. His 1940 helicopter design, the F-282 Kolibri ("hummingbird"), was used during World War II as a submarine spotter.

FAR RIGHT: Igor Ivanovich Sikorsky (1889–1972) lived to witness the Age of Flight, from the Wright brothers to the first moon landing. Born into an aristocratic Russian family, Sikorsky attended the Naval Academy in St. Petersburg, studied engineering in Paris, and resumed studies at Kiev Polytechnic Institute. He emigrated from Russia to the United States in March 1919 and became a U.S. citizen in 1928.

carry a payload of up to 1,500 pounds (681kg). Focke's new helicopter was designated the Fa-233 Drache ("dragon") and was tested in the spring of 1940. It had a 1,000-horsepower engine and two triple-bladed, thirty-nine-foot (11.9m) rotors. The Drache could reach an altitude of 23,400 feet (7,132m) and fly at speeds up to 115 miles per hour (185kph).

Another German aeronautical engineer, Anton Flettner, was also at work in the early 1930s on a helicopter design. He first built an autogiro—the Fl-184—on which to develop his knowledge of control mechanisms. His design reflected his understanding of the aerodynamic forces at work in vertical flight. Out of this testing came the Fl-265, a helicopter with two counter-rotating rotors driven by a single gearbox.

Flettner improved upon this design with the construction of the Fl-282 Kolibri ("hummingbird"). Small and agile,

the Fl-282 Kolibri exhibited certain flight characteristics and abilities that made it an excellent military aircraft. It could reach speeds of nearly ninety miles per hour (144kph) and altitudes of up to 13,000 feet (3,962m). German officials saw its potential as a submarine spotter, thus making the Kolibri the first helicopter with real practical application.

Watching all of this from the United States was Russian émigré Igor Sikorsky, who was itching to get back into the business of helicopter design. Now a successful aircraft manufacturer, Sikorsky began work on another helicopter. He received a patent in 1935 on a design featuring a single lifting rotor and a small vertical tail rotor. In 1939, the VS-300 was born. Described initially as a "bucking bronco" by one test pilot, the VS-300 still had many control problems to be worked out.

TOP: Igor Sikorsky sits in his VS-300. The VS-300 established an international endurance record for helicopter flight on May 6, 1941, staying aloft for 1 hour, 32.4 minutes.

BOTTOM: The Sikorsky R-4 was the result of aggressive testing and development in 1942 by Igor Sikorsky's team of engineers based in Stratford, Connecticut. The experimental versions established numerous aviation records before the final design was put into production for use by the U.S. Army, making the R-4 the first helicopter in the world to be mass-produced. A total of 131 R-4s were produced during World War II, fifty-two of which were sold to Britain's Royal Air Force for rescue operations over the English Channel.

TOP: A Sikorsky VS-300 equipped with pontoons and a covered fuselage. Sikorsky's most important design innovation was the addition of a tail rotor. Its function was to counteract torque created by the main rotor.

BOTTOM: After World War II, the commercial future for helicopters was explored. The S-51 was the civilian version of the R-5 (used in wartime as a rescue helicopter). Shown here on its first flight, on February 16, 1946, the S-51 was used for many practical purposes, including mail delivery.

In 1940, Sikorsky was contracted to build an experimental helicopter (the XR-4) for the U.S. Army Air Corps. Designs for the XR-4 and modifications to the VS-300 moved along simultaneously. Sikorsky and his designers finally realized that two changes could solve their control problems in the VS-300. First, instead of mounting the tail rotors on two outriggers, better handling resulted when a single horizontal propeller was mounted on the tail boom. Second, they discovered the benefits of putting control into the main rotor, using cyclic pitch changes. These and other modifications were tested on the VS-300 in late 1941 and were implemented successfully on the larger XR-4 by the beginning of 1942.

As the war in Europe hobbled German manufacturers Focke and Flettner, Sikorsky prospered. By the end of the war, four hundred Sikorsky helicopters had been manufactured for military use. The YR-4 (the production version of the XR-4) was not widely used during World War II, but it was credited with flying the first wartime search-and-rescue mission, in the jungles of Burma. This event was the beginning of a long and lasting love affair between the military and the helicopter.

Landing a helicopter on an aircraft carrier is a routine event for any naval aviator, but landing one on the small deck of a submarine is a rarity and demands a steady hand.

HOW THEY FLY

When asked "How do helicopters fly?" one youthful pilot smiled and said, "By magic!" Helicopter flight may seem like magic, but like all aircraft, the helicopter must obey the laws of physics and aerodynamics. The way the helicopter manages these laws is what gives it its unique flying characteristics.

A helicopter is a flying machine with a rotary wing. This wing has an airfoil that gives it lift like the wing of a fixed-wing airplane. Unlike a fixed-wing aircraft, which needs forward motion to generate lift, the helicopter's rotor generates lift whether the aircraft is stationary or moving. This is why a helicopter can hover.

PREVIOUS PAGE: While holding a steady hover over the deck of a moving aircraft carrier, the pilot of this U.S. Navy Sea King goes through his final checklist prior to going on station as the ship's plane guard. In the helicopter's open side door, the crew chief (on the right) and rescue swimmer keep their attention focused on the deck below.

RIGHT: The main rotor provides the lifting force for a helicopter. The blades attach to the hub, which provides the mechanical connection to the engine and the mechanisms that allow changes in blade pitch. The rotor on this Russian Mi-26 Halo is the largest in the world, with a diameter of 105 feet (32m). The Halo is also the first helicopter to successfully use an eight-bladed main rotor.

The most common type of helicopter is a conventional helicopter. It has a single main rotor on a vertical shaft. At the end of the tail boom is a tail rotor with an axis of rotation that is approximately ninety degrees to the main rotor. The engine that powers the main rotor also powers the tail rotor by means of a shaft. The cockpit is located in the forward section of the fuselage, ahead of the rotor.

★ MAIN ROTOR ★

In order for an object to leave the ground, it must have a lifting force greater than its weight. The lifting force in a helicopter is generated by the large rotating blades of the main rotor. The shape of each blade is similar to that of the wing of a fixed-wing aircraft. Airflow across the wing, or blade, creates lift. Lift can be increased by either increasing the speed of the rotor or increasing the pitch (angle of attack) of the blade.

Varying the speed of the rotor is more difficult to do than changing the pitch. The rotating mass carries a substantial amount of inertia that is difficult to alter. It is therefore simpler to keep the revolutions per minute (rpm) of the rotor constant and change the pitch, or angle, of the blade. A slight upward tilt of the leading edges of all blades will considerably increase the amount of lift. This lift is controlled by the collective pitch lever to the left of the pilot's seat. Pulling up on the collective pitch lever, called adding collective, increases the amount of pitch on all blades of the main rotor. This in turn creates lift, and the helicopter rises.

★ TAIL ROTOR ★

The tail rotor is a smaller propeller mounted on the rear of the fuselage, or tail boom. It is driven by the helicopter's engine through a series of gears and shafts. The speed of the tail rotor is directly proportional to the speed of the main rotor. The thrust generated by the tail rotor is what counteracts the torque generated by the main rotor. This keeps the helicopter from spinning out of control. The pitch of the tail rotor blades is controlled by the pilot's foot pedals. Whenever there is an increase or decrease in torque created by the main rotor, it

FOLLOWING PAGE: The helicopter's tail rotor (foreground) is angled approximately ninety degrees to the axis of the main rotor, and its speed is proportional to the speed of the main rotor. The vertical boom on which the tail rotor is mounted adds directional stability to a helicopter in forward flight. This helicopter also has a small horizontal stabilizer.

must be compensated for with input to the tail rotor via the foot pedals.

★ FOOT PEDALS ★

The foot pedals are often called yaw pedals in a helicopter. Foot pedals control the direction of flight by controlling the amount of thrust developed by the tail rotor. Pushing on the left pedal will yaw the nose around to the left, and pushing on the right pedal will yaw the nose to the right. It's this balancing act between these two pedals that keeps the helicopter pointed in the desired direction of flight. The harder the pedal is pushed, the more rapidly the helicopter will turn. All controls in a helicopter must be seamlessly coordinated for smooth flight.

★ CYCLICAL CONTROL ★

The cyclic control is a stick situated between the pilot's legs. It controls the helicopter's direction of flight. This is accomplished by adding additional pitch to selected portions of the rotating main rotor. Increasing the pitch in one area will increase lift in that portion, and the rotor disc will tilt. If the cyclic control stick is pushed forward, the pitch will increase only on the rotor blades at the rear of the rotor disc. This will increase lift on the rear portion of the rotor disc and lift up the rear of the rotor, effectively pushing the helicopter forward. Conversely, if the stick is pulled back, it will increase the pitch of the blades at the forward portion of the rotor disc and the helicopter will fly backward. The cyclic control is also what makes it possible for a helicopter to fly sideways.

★ HOVERING ★

A helicopter pilot once likened the difficulty of maintaining a hover to trying to run as fast as you can while holding an empty pizza pan in one hand and balancing a ball bearing dead center in the pan as you go. When a helicopter is hovering, the pilot appears to be making very few perceptible adjustments to the controls, and the aircraft appears to be floating

still in midair. Actually, the pilot is making many small adjustments to the controls. Holding a helicopter in a hover is a difficult feat.

A helicopter takes off for flight from a hover. The hover demands the most power from a helicopter. As the pilot pulls up on the collective pitch control, the aircraft will begin to get light and start to move about, even before it leaves the ground. Input is needed from all controls to keep the helicopter under control—even though it hasn't left the ground.

Once free of the ground and in a hover, the pilot makes constant minute adjustments to all controls. The pilot uses visual cues from his surrounding environment to establish position. This position relative to the ground is maintained using the cyclic stick. Altitude is maintained using the collective pitch control, and heading (direction of flight) is maintained via the foot pedals. In a low hover, the helicopter is aided by the cushion of air created by the main rotor's down-

This Bell LongRanger (identifiable by three side windows) is hovering above the helipad just prior to going out on patrol. The large spotlight under the nose is a Night Sun.

RIGHT: Landing on the rolling, pitching deck of a ship takes concentration by the pilot. Deck crew members stand by to chock the wheels and tie down this Kaman H-2 Seasprite as soon as it lands. Until recently, the H-2 (also known as the LAMPS 1) was used in limited numbers by the U.S. Navy.

OPPOSITE: Flying a helicopter, in this case a U.S. Navy Sikorsky H-3 Sea King, is a multifaceted, hands-on activity. It takes coordination of the collective pitch, in the pilot's left hand, and the cyclic control, in the pilot's right hand, to keep the craft aloft. The pilot's feet are resting on the foot pedals, ready to apply a little pressure to counteract the torque of the rotor. The copilot, on the left, monitors the aircraft's instruments and scans the horizon for other air traffic.

force against the tarmac. This is known as "ground effect." As the altitude increases, ground effect quickly begins to dissipate.

"Transitioning to hover takes a lot of coordination," says veteran Navy helicopter pilot LCDR Jeff Hogan. "It takes a quick eye scan to get all the visual cues. It takes a lot of cyclic input as well. Both your feet are moving, your right hand with the cyclic is moving, and the collective is just maintaining the altitude. It's a coordinated maneuver—you don't just pull up on the collective and freeze the cyclic. As you pull up and get a little light, you can feel the movement of the aircraft in the seat of your pants. So you start compensating for that even before the aircraft leaves the ground. The whole time you're using your visual cues to know if you have any drift."

Any increase in altitude is achieved with additional collective pitch. Easing the cyclic stick in any direction will cause the aircraft to move in that direction, even backward. Any adjustment to one control demands input from the others to compensate in some way. Hovering into the wind is preferred, since the helicopter fuselage tends to "weathervane." It's also easier to hover into the wind because the wind over the spinning rotor blades provides additional lift. Hovering is an incredibly tricky balancing act that looks entirely effortless when done well.

★ TRANSITION TO LEVEL FLIGHT ★

The transition from a hover to level flight is the most hazardous maneuver in helicopter piloting. During this transition, the helicopter leaves a relatively safe position at low altitude as well as the cushion of air created by ground effect. A power failure during a low hover could cause a serious, though probably not fatal, accident.

The shift to forward flight from a hover places the aircraft into an area of transition. The forward motion and resultant increased airflow over the main rotor's blades create lift. This is accomplished by adding collective a fraction of a second prior to pushing the cyclic stick forward. Pushing the cyclic forward lifts the rear of the main rotor disc and pushes the nose down slightly. Collective is added to keep the aircraft from nosing in. Whenever collective is added, there is a torque reaction that must be compensated for via input to the foot pedals. As the helicopter accelerates forward, it will maintain level flight or climb slightly. As the helicopter's forward speed is increased, the cyclic control stick is eased back.

Unlike a fixed-wing aircraft, which can be trimmed for hands-off flying, a helicopter requires full hands-on concentration to fly in all situations. This makes flying a helicopter more physically demanding than flying a fixed-wing aircraft. The constant vibration generated by a helicopter is also something the pilot must learn to live with.

RIGHT: Over the years, Hueys have proven to be versatile and adaptable. Usually seen in shades of olive drab, this U.S. Navy rescue Huey is painted in high-visibility International Orange and white. The pilot has successfully made the transition from a hover to level flight.
OPPOSITE: With tandem seating for the pilot and gunner, the Huey Cobra set the design standard for future attack helicopters. The pilot sits in the rear, slightly elevated above the gunner. Tandem seating gives the Cobra a very narrow fuselage, making it a smaller target. Here, the pilot maintains a low hover over the tarmac.

U.S. MILITARY HELICOPTERS

The earliest documented use of a helicopter in the military was the rescue of a downed pilot who crashed in the jungles of Burma late in 1945. The rescue wasn't a simple task. A nearby hilltop had to be leveled to allow the Sikorsky R-4 to land. The Sikorsky R-4's engine produced 185 horsepower—all of which was needed to carry the helicopter's maximum payload of 530 pounds (240.6kg). Also in 1945, an Army R-5 was assigned to rescue two sailors on a stricken oil barge off the coast of Long Island, New York. This helicopter was equipped with an experimental winch-style rescue hoist. The hoist had been developed during the late phases of the war, and this was its first true test in action.

Both of these events heralded the helicopter's potential. By 1947, more than seventy companies were diligently developing helicopters. Improvements in powerplants and in airframe design expanded the helicopter's role in the military. Following the Korean War, the helicopter was used for transport and search and rescue. In the next decade, halfway around the world, the helicopter would be reborn as an offensive weapon.

The helicopter left its indelible mark on military history during the Vietnam War. Due to the heat, humidity, and jungle terrain, the earliest machines were barely able to safely complete their missions. These troop transports were flying in conditions and in roles for which they were never intended.

Necessity and in-the-field ingenuity led to the modification of many of these choppers so that they might better suit their missions. Back home, aerospace engineers were working overtime to build helicopters with improved capabilities: longer range, larger payload, higher speed, and the capacity to carry weapons. By the mid-1960s, the fresh olive drab paint on the new machines was being soiled in war.

The lessons learned in Vietnam brought about a generation of more lethal helicopters for the 1980s and beyond. The new choppers were more powerful, offered more crew protection, and carried a wide assortment of weapons. Some of the people working the hardest to improve the helicopters' capabilities were electrical and computer engineers designing smaller, highly sophisticated processors. These advanced electronics, along with the new generation of weapons, make today's helicopter a formidable foe.

U.S. taxpayers have certainly gotten their money's worth for the helicopters purchased for military use. The designs have proven to be flexible, allowing easy reconfiguration to suit new missions. The airframes have proven to be structurally sound, providing a very long service life. These helicopters have adapted well to new technologies and have been upgraded, improving performance with new, more powerful engines and sophisticated digital avionics. The speed, agility, and cargo-carrying capabilities of the helicopter have shifted the balance in many combat situations and have saved the lives of many soldiers who otherwise would have been lost due to severe battlefield wounds.

Lessons learned in Vietnam regarding the capabilities of helicopters designed specifically for an attack role led to the development of the AH-64 Apache.

★ B 47 ★

The Bell 47 was arguably the first successful commercial/military helicopter. It first flew in 1945 and is still being flown today. The Bell 47 was a simple, light flying machine. Only a small amount of sheetmetal was used to support the large Plexiglas bubble around the cockpit area. The fuselage framework was exposed, and the tail boom was a triangulated web of tubing. At the end of the boom was a two-bladed tail rotor whose lower portion was protected by an arc of tubing that doubled as a tail skid. Two skids under the fuselage provided the support while on the ground. The two-bladed main rotor is thirty-one feet, seven inches (9.6m) in diameter and is powered by a Lycoming 280-horsepower gasoline engine.

The Bell 47 was the first full-fledged military helicopter hero. Beginning in 1950, it was used extensively in Korea to transport wounded soldiers to MASH (mobile Army surgical hospital) units. The Bell 47 was equipped with two outboard stretchers, one above each landing skid. Each stretcher had a Plexiglas bubble that covered the wounded soldier's upper body. The pilot also acted as in-flight medic, trying to calm the wounded while flying toward the nearest MASH unit. Helicopter rides to a MASH unit were reserved for the most severely wounded. By land, a trip from the battlefield across the rugged Korean terrain to the nearest MASH unit could take as long as twelve hours. The sturdy Bell 47 could deliver these seriously wounded within an hour. Many lives would have been lost without this air-ambulance service. Unfortunately, a few of the brave pilots were also lost. The Bell 47s carried no armor plating, or defensive or offensive weapons. The pilots were directed not to fly in known hostile territory, but the enemy bullets often found their marks, downing several Bell 47s during the conflict.

Bell 47s were also sold to individuals and to companies as transport and utility aircraft. They were also built under license in Italy and in the United Kingdom. A Bell 47 was the first helicopter to be used by the New York City Police Department. Today, Bell 47s fly most often in agricultural roles as sprayers. For this task they are fitted with pesticide tanks and horizontally mounted sprayers. Their small size, superb visibility, and excellent maneuverability make them ideal choices for this difficult job.

The Bell 47, with its distinctive bubble canopy, was the first widely used helicopter. First flown in 1945, examples of the Bell 47 can still be seen flying today.

ROTOR TALES—TRUE STORIES FROM THE SKY

An H-21 Door Gunner's First Mission in Vietnam

In 1962, nobody was paying much attention to the war in Vietnam. It was a very low-profile event. I'd heard about Vietnam and it sounded interesting. I put it down on my dream sheet as my number one choice and I went over there in October of 1962. I was assigned to the Eighth Transportation Helicopter Company in Qui Nhon. I just loved Vietnam. It was the most adventurous experience imaginable: the element of danger, the exotic physical and cultural climate—I was entranced by the whole thing.

I was an assistant crew chief and aspiring gunner assigned to an aircraft, the H-21. A dogmeat design, the H-21

Being a door gunner on any helicopter is a dangerous job, but in a Piasecki H-21, it was especially dangerous. According to some, enemy bullets were often less lethal than the helicopter itself.

was one of the worst helicopters I can imagine for that place and time. It was shaped like a banana and it flew about as well as a banana. A piston-powered, medium-cargo helicopter, the H-21 had trouble lifting the weight of its own immense powerplant, let alone a single squad of infantry. The humidity and heat and high altitude meant that this thing was dangerously underpowered.

The Eighth Transportation unit [flying H-21s] had been in Vietnam about a year. It was part of the first helicopter experiment in the country. The unit had seen some action and had lost a company commander and some other folks in combat by that time. It had been bloodied. It looked, felt, and smelled like a combat organization. Basically, this unit

flew Vietnamese combat units into operations, deposited them in the woods, or resupplied them in field outposts.

Not long after I arrived, I got to fly my very first mission—a combat assault into a landing zone about fifty or sixty miles [80 km to 95km] away. We flew down the coast to a place called Tui Hoa to pick up the troops. It was a very dramatic experience, full of adrenaline and right out of the movies. Somebody comes in and turns on the lights at 4:00 A.M. Dead black. You get up, take a cold shower, and stumble over to the mess hall. At 5:00 A.M. you go into a little briefing room. They talk about "the mission" and how many "lifts" you were going to carry, and they talk about "the VC" and machine guns and what to do when you get shot down and have to "escape and evade." This was all new to me. The whole thing was exciting.

It started getting light. We grabbed our machine guns and ammunition. There we were in our flak jackets, carrying our pistols and machine guns, M-14s and other backup, the M-2 carb and the little WWII .30-caliber. Everybody took all of this very seriously, no kidding around. We loaded the gear onto the aircraft. The pilots came out. And at the precise, appointed hour, we began to crank. Twelve reciprocating engines all began to turn and fire up at the same second. Blue smoke everywhere. From dead silence to thundering noise. It was great. The helicopter started to rock and roll and shimmy as the blades began to turn. It seemed to take forever for the engines to warm up and for the pilots to go through their checklists. Finally, the lead aircraft began to taxi out, followed by number two. All twelve waddled out

to the end of the runway, a procession of elephants, and took off one by one, each needing a running start to get off the ground in almost any circumstance. It felt like *Twelve O'Clock High* with helicopters—the most exotic experience imaginable.

The air over the South China Sea was cool and clear. The twelve helicopters flew in a sort of trail formation south along the coast. In about twenty or thirty minutes, we landed on a large, flat coastal area at Tui Hoa. The troops were all ready on a marked area where we picked them up. I don't know if we even shut down, but we picked up the first "stick" [group of soldiers] and flew off into the mountains. As soon as we got back into the mountains, the lead aircraft dropped down and we started flying contour. The idea was to fly at the lowest possible altitude without hitting anything hard enough to knock you out of the air. It was OK to hit trees, just not too hard. At eighty or ninety knots [90 mph or 103 mph (148kph or 167kph)] it seemed like we were doing a million miles an hour. Things just roared past. I was looking for bad guys. I knew we could get shot at, but I couldn't see any bad guys. It was a very theatrical experience to be roaring above the leaves of those trees. I looked around to check the troops. Most of these guys were pretty hardcore—Vietnamese Airborne—carrying Browning automatic rifles, grenades packed everywhere. Once in a while a T-28, a Skyraider, or a Mohawk would come screaming past and fire a rocket. We were roaring along like the "Ride of the Valkyries."

I stuck my head out the door and could see the landing zone ahead. The pilots began to slow down. The landing zones were occupied. The idea was to sequence the aircraft in and out without hovering or orbiting. At last it was our turn. I still hadn't seen anyone I could kill, or who could kill me. We started our approach into the landing zone, a small clearing in the brush. It was open terrain, not jungle, but the trees were twenty feet [6m] high. But there was another helicopter in the landing zone that was slow getting out, so we had to abort our entry. Well, that underpowered, radial engine didn't have the power to do it. The pilots pulled everything they had. We slowly wallowed into the landing zone, and as we sort of crash-landed, nearly meshing blades with the other guy now departed, the aft rotor blades went into the trees. All the Vietnamese troops got out in prompt order, glad to be away from that flying death trap and into safer territory with the Vietcong.

Once rid of them, we pulled pitch and it was obvious right away that there was a problem. The helicopter was vibrating like crazy. The pilots put two and two together and figured they had damage to the rotor blade. We staggered back maybe ten miles [16km], away from the LZ [landing zone]. Another helicopter stayed with us. We landed in a more open area and shut the whole thing down. The crew chief and I climbed up on the back. Those blades were butchered. With me pulling the blades around, the crew chief put 100-mph [161kph] tape over the holes, which were six inches [15.2cm] or eight inches [20.3cm] across. We gaffer-taped the damn thing. Then we fired up and flew home. So that was my introduction to combat. It was a liberating adventure and the perfect antidote to twelve years of elementary and high school. I didn't see anything and nobody shot me—it was thrilling!

I was lucky to have been there in 'sixty-two and 'sixty-three. The VC didn't shoot very well and there weren't very many of them. Compared to what the guys went through in 'sixty-five and later, it was a piece of cake. They would have laughed. So I remember my tour of duty with great affection. I actually thought the most dangerous part of the operation was the helicopter itself. It scared me. I was not afraid of getting shot. I got more and more afraid of the H-21 killing me. It was a dangerous thing to ride around in. The longer I did it the more uncomfortable I got—very uncomfortable.

—Hans Halberstadt

Hans Halberstadt has been photographing and writing about all types of military and civil aviation for thirty-five years. He still enjoys taking a ride in a military aircraft whenever he can. Today, he shoots with a Nikon instead of a machine gun.

ABOVE: Early in the Vietnam War, the Piasecki H-21 was the primary troop transport helicopter. A group of soldiers makes a hasty exit as the H-21's rotors blow over rice stalks in their wake. The weight of the large helicopter has buried the main landing gear deep in the rice paddy.

OPPOSITE: This U.S. Marine Corps Huey has dropped off a load of troops using a technique called "fast roping." The troops have slid down the ropes and are running for cover. The crew is casting off the ropes in preparation for a rapid departure.

★ PIASECKI H-21 ★

The Piasecki H-21 Workhorse was designed and built by the Piasecki Helicopter Company in Morton, Pennsylvania. The first prototype was flown in April 1952. On August 26, 1956, an H-21 became the first helicopter to make a nonstop transcontinental helicopter flight across the United States.

Often called the Flying Banana because of its unique shape, the H-21 was the first successful twin-rotor helicopter. It was powered by a single Wright nine-cylinder radial piston engine that developed 1,425 horsepower. The engine was in the rear of the fuselage, which helped to balance the helicopter's weight. Both of the H-21's three-bladed rotors were forty-four feet, nine inches (13.6m) in diameter. They rotated in opposite directions to counteract torque. The empty weight of the H-21 was 8,000 pounds (3,632kg), and maximum gross weight at takeoff was 13,300 pounds (5,902kg). The twin vertical stabilizers aided directional stability in forward flight. The H-21 operated with a crew of two and could carry fourteen soldiers or twelve stretchers. A 5,000-pound (2,270kg) load could be slung underneath. Cruising speed was a slow ninety-eight miles per hour (157.7kph) at sea level.

The U.S. Army took delivery of its first H-21 in June 1961. The initial contract called for 334 H-21s. They were assigned to troop transport and cargo duties. The army's H-21s saw duty in the early days of the Vietnam conflict, transporting ARVN (Army of the Republic of Vietnam) troops into and out of combat zones. Underpowered for Vietnam's harsh conditions of heat and humidity, they were replaced by the turbine-powered Hueys in 1963.

★ UH-1 HUEY ★

Its official name is UH-1A Iroquois, but this designation is rarely used. It's simply called the Huey. The name "Huey" was derived from its original military designation of HU-1 ("H" for "helicopter," "U" for "utility"). This designation was later changed to UH-1, but "Huey" stuck. The Huey has become an icon of the Vietnam War. Its sound is as distinctive as its chubby appearance. The Huey is the most successful and widely used helicopter in the U.S. military inventory. More than seven thousand Bell UH-1 Hueys have been built in many different configurations. It is the highest-production aircraft since the end of World War II and is still being built in Japan.

The UH-1A was originally designed as a light-utility helicopter, which Bell designed to meet the U.S. Army's specifications for the XH-40 (X = experimental; H = helicopter) program. The first of the 182 production A models were delivered in 1959. The Huey's first overseas military service was in 1962 in Vietnam, when the UH-1A was used by the Army as an air ambulance.

The Huey was the first production helicopter powered by a gas turbine engine. Its Lycoming T33 engine produced 770 horsepower and was an adequate powerplant to lift the A model Huey's design weight of 5,210 pounds (2,365kg). The A version was designed to carry either three stretchers or four troops in addition to its crew of three: pilot, copilot, and crew chief. Lycoming later increased the horsepower of the T33 to 1,000. This increased the payload to six stretchers or twelve combat-ready troops in addition to the crew. By the time domestic production ceased in 1987, the Huey was powered by a 1,400-horsepower engine. Its capabilities, reliability, and longevity had exceeded all expectations by the time it had finished its evolution.

The Huey picked up in Vietnam where the Bell 47 left off in Korea—as an air ambulance in the service of saving the lives of the most seriously wounded. Because of the nature of the battlefronts and Vietnam's terrain, Hueys often had to evade enemy bullets to pick up injured soldiers. The Huey could

In Vietnam, the Huey helicopters used for medical evacuation were given the call sign Dustoff. Flying without defensive weapons, these air ambulances saved hundreds of lives by evacuating wounded soldiers from the battlefield to MASH units.

By autumn 1965, air mobility had come to dominate the mode of battle in Vietnam. The United States had committed large numbers of ground troops, and hundreds of Hueys replaced the H-21s. Massive air assaults were carried out where U.S. ground troops took on the role of tracking down and engaging the enemy. During larger-scale operations, as many as eight Huey gunships escorted the unarmed Slicks into areas of suspected Vietcong activity. In advance of the Hueys, Air Force fighters usually prepped the area with a variety of rockets and bombs. As soon as the fighters departed, Huey gunships rolled into the area to further soften up the LZ. Their mission was to defend against any possible ambush of the approaching troop carriers.

As the Slicks came in and landed, gunships were arrayed on either side of the transport chopper. Once the Slicks were on the ground, the gunships circled. It was their job to make sure the Slicks and their exiting troops were not assaulted. As the Slicks were departing, the gunships would remain on-station for close support of the ground soldiers. It wasn't unusual for gunships to engage enemy forces who were in close proximity to the friendly forces that had just landed. The Vietcong would often establish well-concealed gun emplacements around likely LZs. They would remain hidden until the Slicks were on the ground and troops were being unloaded. Then the VC would open up in a deadly crossfire. The gunships would then roll in in multiple teams in trail formation. As the first ship broke off the target, the following ship would start its firing pass. The strategy was to keep a constant field of suppressive fire on the target area. This was especially important when the lead helicopter was breaking off the target because that's when a helicopter is most vulnerable from ground fire. Huey pilots found that one of their best defenses was flying as low as possible. In Vietnam, it wasn't unusual for a Huey to return to base with tree branches entangled in its landing skids.

One of the most potent Huey gunships was known as the Hog. It was a special version flown by the ARA (Aerial Rocket Artillery). Each of these ARA Hueys carried forty-eight rockets.

carry three wounded on stretchers. A medic attended to their needs while at the controls were a pilot and copilot. The Vietnam medevac (for "medical evacuation") Hueys were assigned the call name Dustoff. The Dustoff Hueys were marked with a traditional large red cross, which more often than not became a target for the enemy. Most Dustoff Hueys flew their missions without defensive armament. The pilots and crew of these choppers were intensely devoted to their missions. Although many Dustoff pilots and crew were killed while trying to rescue their fallen comrades, they were highly successful overall and saved thousands of lives in the process.

Not all Hueys delivered to Vietnam were used for medevac. Some Hueys were also configured as troop transports, commonly called Slicks. The Huey gunships bristled with guns, and the Hogs (which were armed with rockets) were airborne artillery platforms.

The CH-47 Chinook (in background) and the UH-1 Huey were the U.S. Army's two main troop transport helicopters throughout the Vietnam War.

It was the Hog's mission to unleash a great deal of firepower accurately on enemy positions. These choppers were not there to replace standard ground artillery, only to augment it. They could reach enemy emplacements that standard ground artillery couldn't reach. The Hogs would dive in at steep angles and place their rockets precisely on target. Because of the low altitudes and close proximity to the target, Hog pilots had to be careful not to get caught by any fragments from the explosions created by their own rockets.

The Huey gunships and Hogs were a short-term solution to the problem of insufficient air support. They were never designed for the gunship role and suffered many deficiencies, the most serious of which was insufficient speed to keep up with the troop transports. The face of helicopter warfare would soon change with the introduction of the AH-1 Huey Cobra.

Another member of the Huey family worth noting is the UH-1N Iroquois, Twin Huey. It was originally designed and built for the Canadian government. The Twin Huey is powered by two T400-CP-400 Pratt & Whitney (of Canada), Turbo "Twin-Pac" engines. These engines produce 1,800 shaft horsepower and drive through a single transmission. The Twin Huey has been adopted by the U.S. military and can be armed with two General Electric 7.62mm mini-guns or two 40mm grenade launchers. Additionally, two seven-tube 2.75-inch rocket pods can be added. Eight to ten combat-ready troops can be transported, or six litters, if configured as an air ambulance. In civilian dress as the Bell 212, the Twin Huey is used for air rescue, fire fighting, and transport.

Even before the lead Huey's skids touch the ground, the impatient South Vietnamese Second Division soldiers make their way to its door. It can be assumed by the position of each of the Huey's two door-mounted machine guns that this landing zone is in friendly territory.

The U.S. Marine Corps' Super Cobra provides close-in fire support to landing forces during amphibious assaults and subsequent land operations. The Cobra is equipped with a 20mm gun in the nose turret and can carry 2.75-inch and 5-inch rockets, Hellfire and TOW antiarmor missiles, Sidewinder air-to-air missiles, and Sidearm antiradiation missiles.

★ BELL AH-1 HUEY COBRA AND ★ AH-1W SUPER COBRA

Other than the shape of the tail boom, there is little in the appearance of the AH-1G Huey Cobra that shows off its UH-1 Huey lineage. Originally designed in the early 1960s as an escort for troop carriers, this helicopter was subsequently developed into a highly effective weapons platform. Initially it was scheduled only for a short production run, making way for the proposed AH-56 Cheyenne. But when the Cheyenne program was canceled, Bell started work on improved models of the Cobra.

The first flight of a Huey Cobra was in autumn 1965. By March of the following year, Bell received its first order from the U.S. Army. The army liked what it saw. The mechanics (engine and transmission) were borrowed from the Huey. The fuselage was unusually narrow (36 inches [91cm]), with tandem seating for the pilot and weapons officer. Stub wings were added to ease the load on the main rotor and to provide weapons stations.

The Cobra was a fighter plane with a rotary wing. It had a top speed of 219 miles per hour (352kph), nearly double that of the troop carriers it escorted. Its speed came from a new wider main rotor, lighter weight, and streamlined shape. It was exceptionally maneuverable and could carry 3,000 pounds (1,362kg) of armament on the stub wings.

Under the nose was a turret that could mount mini-guns, rapid-firing cannons, or grenade launchers. The turret could pivot in a wide arc to both sides of the helicopter as well as up and down. Movement of the turret was controlled by the weapons officer seated in the front seat. If the turret was locked in the forward position, the pilot in the rear seat could fire it.

The Cobra was powered by a single 1,100-horsepower Lycoming turboshaft engine, like those used in the Huey. The U.S. Marine Corps also ordered its own version, the AH-1J Sea Cobra. The AH-1J Sea Cobra had two Pratt & Whitney engines, the second, backup engine offering additional security during frequent, over-water flights.

The introduction of the Huey Cobra marked a turning point in the development of helicopter technology and its application. Previously, helicopters had been transports fitted with defensive weapons. The Huey Cobra proved that a helicopter could be designed as a purely offensive weapon as well.

The current version of the Cobra is the AH-1W Super Cobra. Specifically, the Super Cobra is designed to provide close-in fire support in both day and night battlefield environments. Its avionics, engines, and weapons systems have all been substantially upgraded to meet the expanded mission parameters.

The Super Cobra is powered by two General Electric T-700-GE-401 engines, each producing 1,725 shaft horsepower. Fuel for these engines is contained within the fuselage in two self-sealing fuel cells with a total capacity of 307 gallons (1kl). Under-wing stores stations provide mounts for up to four additional tanks with a capacity of seventy-seven gallons (291l) each.

The two-bladed main rotor is forty-eight feet (14.6m) in diameter. The blades have an aluminum spar and aluminum-faced honeycomb aft of the spar. The tail rotor is constructed of aluminum honeycomb with a stainless steel skin and leading edge. Future improvements to the Super Cobra call for a four-bladed main rotor, which will reduce vibration by seventy percent.

Like the original Huey Cobra, the Super Cobra has a crew of two seated in tandem. The pilot sits in the rear seat, which is slightly elevated above the forward-seated copilot/gunner. The cockpit is climate-controlled with both heat and air conditioning. Even though the Super Cobra is piloted from the rear seat, there is a full set of flight controls in the front cockpit. Both cockpits are surrounded with armor protection. The interior lighting and pilot's heads-up display are compatible with night-vision goggles. The Super Cobra is fitted with a night targeting system, which includes a FLIR (forward-looking infrared), a low-light television camera, Laser Designation Range Finder, and an autotrack system installed in the existing TOW (tube-launched, optically tracked, wire-guided) missile.

The Super Cobra has an electrically operated chin turret that houses a three-barrel 20mm machine gun. Storage for the gun's 750 rounds of ammunition is directly behind the turret. The firing rate of this cannon is 675 rounds per minute, but

The chin turret on the AH-1W Super Cobra houses an electrically operated three-barrel 20mm gun. This gun fires at a rate of 675 rounds per minute. Above the turret is the night targeting system's FLIR, low-light television, and laser designation range finder.

there is a sixteen-round burst limiter on the firing switch. This turret can track 110 degrees to each side of the aircraft, 18 degrees up, and 50 degrees down. The five-foot (1.5m) length of the barrel makes it necessary for the Super Cobra's turret to be pointing forward when firing wing stores.

The stub wing stores stations can be configured to carry a wide variety of lethal air-to-air or air-to-ground weapons. Attachments are available that enable the mounting of four nineteen-tube or four seven-tube 2.75-inch rocket launcher pods. Also mountable on the underwing stores stations are several types of flare dispensers, grenade dispensers, and minigun pods. Significant to the Super Cobra's role against tanks is the mounting of both Hellfire and TOW missiles (up to eight each). The Canadian Marconi TOW/Hellfire control system enables the Super Cobra to fire both the TOW and Hellfire on the same mission. Sidewinder air-to-air missiles or Sidearm antiradiation missiles can be mounted on the outboard stations. Under consideration as a future weapon for the Super Cobra is the air-to-surface Maverick missile.

During Operation Desert Storm, the U.S. Marine Corps deployed four of its six active force squadrons. Forty-eight AH-1Ws saw action in the Persian Gulf War. The Super Cobras destroyed ninety-seven tanks, 104 armored personnel carriers, sixteen bunkers, and two antiaircraft sites without losing a single aircraft.

One of the best friends a ground soldier can have is a Cobra helicopter hovering nearby. These ground troops are on the radio coordinating enemy positions with the Cobra.

★ BOEING VERTOL CH-47 CHINOOK ★

In 1956, the design of the U.S. Army's all-weather medium transport began. At that time the army was concerned with a possible conflict in Central Europe. Specifications for the new helicopter included a cargo ramp at the rear, through which light vehicles could be loaded. Seating was required for forty combat troops. In addition, the new helicopter had to be able to transport a 16,000-pound (7,264kg) load slung underneath. Vertol, one of five companies submitting proposals, suggested an enlarged version of the U.S. Navy's Sea Knight. In 1959, an order was placed for five flying prototypes of the large load–carrying chopper. The prototype YCH-47A flew on September 21, 1961. Following a successful flight test program, the first CH-47A Chinooks were assigned to the U.S.

Army's 1st Cavalry Division. In 1965, these units were deployed to Vietnam.

The first Chinook model was the CH-47A. It was powered by two Lycoming T55-L-7 turboshaft engines, each producing 2,650 horsepower. Two engines were mounted on the exterior of the rear fuselage, just below the rear rotor. A combining gearbox drove both rotors. Two sixty-foot (18.3m) -diameter three-bladed rotors turned in opposite directions. These rotors could be folded when the Chinook was transported aboard a ship or inside a transport aircraft.

The Chinook's fuselage is an all-metal monocoque construction with aluminum and Fiberglas external panels. The bottom half of the fuselage is sealed for missions that would take the Chinook to water level (such as delivering or recovering a Special Forces team). Along each side of the fuselage,

The interior of a CH-47 Chinook is cavernous. Seats are mounted along both bulkheads, allowing the Chinook to carry as many as fifty-five combat troops. To transport cargo, the seats can be removed. Tie-down rings in the floor are used to secure cargo.

sealed rounded pods provide additional buoyancy. The Chinook's landing gear is a nonretractable quadracycle type. Each front unit has twin wheels, with single wheels on each rear. The rear cargo ramp can be lowered when the Chinook is in the air, inches above the water, or on the ground.

The Chinook is flown by a crew of three: pilot, copilot, and crew chief, who sits on a jump seat directly behind the two flight officers. One or more load masters are typically part of the air crew, depending on the size of the load.

Following their 1965 arrival in Vietnam, Chinooks were used as troop and cargo transports. In 1966, three specially built CH-47 gunships were tested by the 1st Cavalry Division. These particular Chinooks were known as Go-Go Birds. They were probably the most potent and heavily armed helicopters in the war. Each Go-Go could be armed with a wide variety of weapons systems. The primary armament consisted of a 40mm grenade launcher mounted in an undernose turret. The Go-Go also had two stub wings, each mounting a 20mm cannon. In addition to the two 20mm cannons, either two nineteen-tube rocket pods or two mini-guns can be added. Bristling out of the Go-Go Bird's windows were five .50-caliber machine guns. A number of these Chinooks were also employed as bombers to punish underground fortifications and tunnel systems. During these operations, fifty-five-gallon (208l) drums of tear gas were rolled out the back of the Chinook in an attempt to drive the burrowed Vietcong above ground. Napalm was also rigged and dropped out the back. A single Chinook could devastate a target with two and a half tons (2,270kg) of napalm. The Go-Go Birds generally performed traditional, close support missions for ground soldiers. They had incredible endurance and maximum firepower, which allowed them to neutralize every enemy position during the evaluation period. Ultimately, the program was canceled as the Chinooks were desperately needed for troop transport. Besides, a new attack helicopter was on its way to Vietnam—the Huey Cobra.

Throughout its lifetime, the Chinook has been upgraded several times. Each successive model (B and C) was given more powerful engines; the B model received improved rotor blades.

The version being flown today by the U.S. Army is the CH-47D. Older versions are being rebuilt to new specifications. The CH-47D upgrade entails stripping the aircraft down to a bare airframe. The structure and skin are repaired and refurbished. Two Allied Signal T-55-L-712 turboshaft engines are fitted with updated transmissions and cooling. The rotor blades are composite material, strong enough to take a hit from a 23mm armor-piercing round. The CH-47D's flight deck will be compatible with night-vision goggles. A redundant electrical system and new avionics will be installed as a safeguard against failure of either. The CH-47D will have an advanced automatic flight control system. Externally, the D models will differ from the previous models only by virtue of a rectangular intake to draw air into the front of the rear rotor

pylon for oil coolers. Some D models have been fitted with air-to-air refueling probes.

The CH-47Ds are considerably lighter than previous models. This reduction in weight is due to the use of composite materials and compact electronics equipment. At its maximum gross takeoff weight of 50,000 pounds (22,700kg), the Chinook D has more than double the load capacity of the original A model. Test loads on a Chinook D included an M198 155mm howitzer, thirty-two rounds of ammunition for the howitzer, and an eleven-man crew. The total internal and external cargo weight was 22,000 pounds (9,988kg). Also hauled in a test run was a Caterpillar D5 bulldozer, supported by only the center cargo hook, that weighed a whopping 24,750 pounds (11,237kg).

OPPOSITE: In addition to transporting troops, the Chinook can also transport vehicles and artillery to and from the battlefield. The soldier standing on the vehicle is about to attach it to the CH-47's center cargo hook. **RIGHT:** The Chinook's two turboshaft engines are mounted on the rear of the fuselage, one on either side of the rear rotor's pylon. The engines turn through a gearbox that drives both rotors. The large cargo door in the rear facilitates loading of either troops or cargo.

The U.S. Army Special Forces have their own version of the Chinook, the MH-47E. Its mission profile requires that it fly a five-and-a-half-hour, deep-penetration mission over a 345-mile (555km) radius in adverse weather, day or night, and in all terrain conditions. To meet this mission, the MH-47E is powered by upgraded T-55-L-714 engines and has extra fuel capacity. Terrain-following radar allows flight as low as 100 feet (30m). The E model has a FLIR system that is mounted in a chin turret. Armament includes Stinger missiles, which use FLIR for sighting, and a window-mounted machine gun on each side of the aircraft.

Boeing has proposed an Improved Cargo Helicopter configuration for use by the U.S. Army, a program involving the development and production of a new Chinook version. Benefits of the improved Chinook include reduced vibration to increase airframe and systems reliability. Also planned are reduced pilot workload and more efficient cargo handling. This new version would remain operational from 2015 to 2020. At that time, an entirely new, yet-to-be-designed cargo helicopter should be entering U.S. Army service.

★ BOEING VERTOL CH-46 SEA KNIGHT ★

The twin-rotor concept so effectively used in the Piasecki HRP-1 spawned several new designs. One of those was the CH-46 Sea Knight built by the Vertol Corporation, which was subsequently purchased by Boeing; the combined entity is now known as Boeing Vertol. The Sea Knight first flew in 1958 and was designed for both military and civilian use. The U.S. Army tested early models and found them too small for its needs. It settled on Vertol's larger CH-47 Chinook. The U.S. Navy and Marine Corps found the Sea Knight very suitable as a medium helicopter. It would be assigned to troop transport, utility, and cargo.

When the U.S. Navy and Marine Corps ordered their first Sea Knights, in 1961, they requested a more powerful pair of General Electric GE-8B engines, which produced 1,250 horsepower each. By 1965, these early A models would see active duty with the Marines in Vietnam.

Following a training mission, three U.S. Marine Corps CH-46 Sea Knight helicopters land on an airfield at Camp Pendleton, California. The helicopter in the foreground carries a desert camouflage paint scheme, while the other two are in shades of low-vis gray. Each of these Sea Knights is equipped with two .50-caliber machine guns.

The CH-46 is very similar in appearance to the Army's CH-47 Chinook. One major difference is the Sea Knight's tricycle landing gear and slightly smaller overall size.

The Sea Knight is a twin-rotor medium-lift helicopter. The twin three-bladed fifty-one-foot (15.5m)-diameter rotors counteract torque by spinning in opposite directions. The current CH-46E models all use the General Electric T58-GE-16 engines. Each of these engines is rated at 1,870 horsepower, and each is mounted on top of the rear fuselage at the base of the rear rotor pylon. The forward rotor, which is just above the cockpit, is driven by a high-speed driveshaft that runs inside a tunnel along the top of the fuselage. In an emergency, the Sea Knight can be flown on one engine.

The Sea Knight's large cabin can accommodate twenty-five combat-ready troops on fold-down canvas seats. Up to fifteen litters can be fitted when the chopper is used for medevac. The Sea Knight's wide rear ramp facilitates loading of troops or cargo.

To allow water landings, the Sea Knight's cabin is sealed. The large main gear sponsons provide flotation when the Sea Knight is brought down to water level. To remain fully stable at water level, the rotors must remain turning. A typical water-level mission for a Sea Knight would be the deployment or retrieval of U.S. Navy SEAL teams.

When deployed as a Marine troop transport or SEAL team delivery vehicle, the Sea Knight can be lightly armed. A .50-caliber machine gun can be mounted just aft of the cockpit in the starboard door. It's typically the crew chief's responsibility to man this gun.

The Gulf War provided an excellent opportunity for the aging Sea Knight to prove its worth. In that theater, it served as the U.S. Navy's principal replenishment aircraft. Logging more than 15,000 hours of service, the Navy's Sea Knights lifted ninety tons (81,720kg) of cargo, two tons (1,816kg) of mail, and more than 37,000 passengers. These accomplishments are amplified by the fact that the Sea Knight maintained an 87-percent mission-capable status. The Sea Knight is one of those marvelous examples of a timeless design that remains in active service today (with both the U.S. Navy and Marines), nearly forty years after its introduction.

★ MCDONNELL DOUGLAS AH-64 APACHE ★

The McDonnell Douglas AH-64 Apache is a natural-born tank killer. Named in honor of the proud Apache warrior, the AH-64 was the first day/night, all-weather helicopter designed specifically as an armor crusher.

Following the Vietnam War, the U.S. Army realized it needed a helicopter designed specifically for an attack role. Several manufacturers submitted design proposals for a new helicopter. One of the companies to submit a proposal was Hughes Helicopter, which, in 1984, became McDonnell Douglas Helicopter Company. In 1976, the Hughes YAH-64 prototype was chosen from the proposals submitted. In September 1983, the first Apache rolled out of the Hughes factory. Following an extensive flight and evaluation period, the first delivery was made to the U.S. Army on January 26, 1984. The last of the AH-64As was delivered to the Army in November 1996. In total, the U.S. Army purchased 937 AH-64A Apaches.

The Apache's first combat missions were flown in Panama during Operation Just Cause. Eleven AH-64s were deployed for that conflict. More recently, 288 Apaches were used extensively against Iraq during the 1991 Gulf War. The Apaches took part in the war's first air strike. During that war, their tank-destroying exploits were well documented each evening on network and cable news television broadcasts.

The new Apache was an all-business, no-frills design. What it lacked in aesthetics it made up for in performance. Its overall length is fifty-one feet (15.5m), and it weighs 11,387 pounds (5,170kg) empty. Small stub wings are mounted on the fuselage just rearward of the cockpit. These wings provide a small amount of lift and, more important, serve as multiple mounting points for external stores pylons. External fuel tanks can also be mounted on these minimal wings. Below the tail rotor is a horizontal tail plane commonly called a stabilator.

The Apache is powered by twin General Electric T-700-GE-701 turboshaft engines producing a total shaft horsepower of 3,392. The Apache's two engines are mounted six feet,

This AH-64 Apache is concealed in the trees, waiting for its opportunity to attack. This tactic requires a skilled pilot to nestle the Apache's 48-foot (14.6m) diameter rotor in amongst the foliage. From this overhead view, the engine's exhaust deflectors can clearly be seen. These deflectors reduce the temperature of the exiting gases, thereby diminishing the Apache's infrared signature.

seven inches (2m) apart to reduce the likelihood of both engines being damaged at the same time by enemy fire. Each of the two main engines has a system that reduces the exhaust temperature from more than 1,000 degrees Fahrenheit (538°C) to less than 600 degrees Fahrenheit (316°C). This is done to diminish the infrared signature to below the range of heat-seeking weapons. This reduction in temperature is accomplished by drawing in external air and mixing it with exhaust gases. A 125-horsepower onboard APU (auxiliary power unit) is used to start the engines. This APU can also be used when the engines are shut down to provide full electrical power, pressurized air, and hydraulic pressure.

The Apache's main rotor is forty-eight feet (14.6m) in diameter. Stainless steel spars and Fiberglas tubes provide the backbone for each of the four blades. The leading edges are covered with stainless steel and can withstand the impact against a two-inch (5cm) -diameter tree branch. The composite trailing edge is durable enough to withstand the hit from a .50-caliber machine gun. The tail rotor is composed of two twin-bladed hubs.

Surrounding the crew and vital aircraft systems is armor plating made of boron carbide bonded to Kevlar. A blast shield separates crew members, reducing the likelihood of one hit eliminating both the pilot and copilot/weapons officer. Armored seats can withstand .50-caliber incendiary armor-piercing rounds. The Apache's fuel cells are located forward and aft of the ammunition bay. They are self-sealing and are filled with nitrogen to reduce the chance of fire, should an incendiary round penetrate the surrounding armor.

Crash survivability was designed into the Apache's crew compartment. The canopy is strong enough to withstand a rollover accident. Both cockpit seats were designed to absorb crash impact. The Apache's airframe is designed to collapse progressively in a crash, increasing the crew's survival chances. The fixed main landing gear is built to be crashworthy and to absorb the impact of a hard landing.

The Apache's armament capability is impressive. Under the cockpit is a 30mm chain gun. Up to 1,200 rounds of

ammunition can be carried to feed this cannon. The 30mm gun is mounted in a turret that can be set to follow the direction in which the weapons officer turns his head. The stub wings are designed to carry sixteen laser-guided Hellfire antitank missiles or seventy-six 2.75-inch folding-fin rockets. A program was initiated in 1987 to integrate the Stinger air-to-air missile into the Apache's arsenal of doom. Evaluation tests were also conducted in which the Sidewinder heat-seeking air-to-air missile was fired from modified Apaches. Multimission flexibility is the key to the Apache helicopter's weapon system.

Following the Gulf War, improvements were introduced to upgrade the Apache's navigation system and radios. New rotor blades were also planned. Scheduled for the upgrade were 254 AH-64As to be designated AH-64B. This program was canceled in 1992. A C model was also planned, but the modi-

fications included what would eventually become the D model. All new or remanufactured Apaches are now designated AH-64D.

The AH-64D is also called the Longbow Apache. It is visibly distinct from the A model by virtue of its mast-mounted radar. The Longbow version is a current joint improvement program with Lockheed Martin and Westinghouse as the principal contractors. The Longbow system consists of a mast-mounted millimeter-wave-length fire-control radar and Longbow Hellfire missile. The Longbow radar detects and acquires ground targets and detects air targets. The system processors receive the radar data. They classify, prioritize, and display the target information on the pilot's display. This system also passes the targeting data on to other aircraft and to the onboard Longbow Hellfire missiles. The pilots may then engage up to sixteen targets in one minute. The new Longbow

Located in the center of the front cockpit is the TADS (Target Acquisition Designation Sight) display. TADS provides the gunner with day and night target acquisition data by means of a direct-view optical telescope, a day television, and FLIR. These sensors may be used singly, or in combination—depending on tactical, weather, and visibility conditions.

Hellfire is a true "fire-and-forget" precision missile. Target data can also be passed via digital links to other weapons systems with compatible digital systems. The Longbow system significantly reduces decision and exposure times—both very important factors in a battlefield situation.

Other significant upgrades to the D model include more powerful General Electric T-700-GE-701C engines, larger generators, a new Doppler navigation system, and a vapor cycle cooling system for the avionics. Not all D models will carry the Longbow radar and fire control systems, but all reworked Apaches will carry the designation AH-64D.

★ SIKORSKY SH-3 SEA KING ★

The Navy's SH-3 Sea King was the first helicopter to combine ASW (antisubmarine warfare) capabilities into a single aircraft. Previously, two SH-34 helicopters were used as an ASW team. The SH-3 was Sikorsky's response to the U.S. Navy's 1957 request for such an aircraft. It first flew in 1959 and was delivered to the Navy's fleet squadrons in 1962. The Sea King was much larger than its H-34 predecessor and much more capable in its multiple roles of ASW, transport, and search and rescue. The Sea King was initially powered by two General Electric

The Apache's crew of two fly and fight together. The pilot sits in the elevated rear cockpit and the copilot/gunner sits in the front. The entire cockpit area is surrounded by armor plating.

ABOVE: Lieutenant Colonel Rick Rife is an eighteen-year veteran of the U.S. Army. During that time, he has flown more than seven hundred hours in the AH-64 Apache and nineteen hundred hours in several other Army helicopters.

OPPOSITE: One of the U.S. Army's most valuable assets during Desert Storm was the AH-64 Apache. Flying both day and night missions, the Apaches systematically destroyed Iraqi armor.

AH-64 Apaches Get Ready for Desert Storm

I deployed to Desert Shield/Desert Storm with an Apache squadron as part of the 2nd Armored Division. The squadron consisted of eighteen Apaches, thirteen OH-58s, and three UH-60s. We arrived in early October, went into port, got our aircraft, reassembled them, and then moved directly out to a field site in the sands of Saudi Arabia. We trained hard all the way through to the outset of the missions for Desert Storm.

The training was much different from what we had done in the States. We had to worry about the threat of SOFs [Special Operations Forces] coming into our line, so we tried to maximize our security. Then we tried to get the pilots acclimated—that was the biggest challenge. Our guys initially had trouble landing in the sand. The rotor wash kicked up so much desert sand that the pilots experienced a "brown out." So we set up a training program to develop and practice a new landing technique. Instead of bringing the aircraft into a hover, we planted it. Here's how it worked. Once you set up your approach, the blowing sand started to engulf the aircraft. You tried to keep it behind you, basically from the pilot on back. To do

that, you had to maintain air speed. Once you got down to the ground, you would lose visibility because you'd brown out. But you continued on with your airspeed and relied on what we refer to as "the system."

By "the system" I mean the pilot's night-vision sensor. It consists of a turret-mounted FLIR located in the aircraft's nose, plus the display of the FLIR image that can be seen on the pilot's helmet-mounted right-eye monocle. The pilot's night-vision system FLIR is slaved to the pilot's helmet. There is nothing actually attached to his head—it's all done with infrared sensors. Wherever the pilot looks, the FLIR will point in that direction, giving him the image. Superimposed on that image is the symbology of the cockpit instruments (altitude, airspeed, and where the weapons systems are pointing). All of that is presented on the monocle. So when the pilot comes in, he flies the symbology that's presented [that is, adjusts the flight controls solely on the basis of the instrument readings that are displayed on the helmet monocle, without the usual "look out the window" visual references]. Basically he lines it up, shoots it, and just keeps it going until he feels contact with the ground.

As we became more accustomed to flying in the desert, we had to modify our tactics from those we flew in the States. At Fort Hood we flew low, over trees and shrubbery. When we got to the desert, we couldn't fly as low due to the blowing sand. Instead we'd go into a hover position from a higher altitude to engage a target. Any lower and we'd brown out from the blowing sand. Other units used "running fire," a tactic where they'd fire while on the move. We stayed with a hover, but only at a higher altitude. The air defense threat was minimal enough that we did not have to be at a low altitude to remain safe. We were also growing accustomed to the flight data that the system was providing at these altitudes. All this took time, from a training perspective.

Many of our pilots had never shot a Hellfire missile. So we had them shoot Hellfire missiles as part of our training. Our crews were stabilized and we didn't have any rotation, so we had a group of pilots who trained hard and we were ready to go. The training was harder than the actual combat. We trained for night missions because it's more demanding to fly and fight at night. Most actual combat missions, though, took place during daylight, so it was somewhat easier than the training.

We eventually got a call that there was possible enemy movement toward our sector. We launched on that, and when we launched, everybody thought, "Hey, this is for real!... Let's go!" We did several of those. We also did the berm-buster operations. One of the brigades was given the mission to go across the berm [the battle line] and feel out the threat. They went across and took some hits and lost a couple of vehicles and some personnel. We were called up to provide support. The average mission we flew was two hours, which is one fuel load with no auxiliary tanks.

The Apache is a phenomenal machine. I think it proved itself over there. That action sold the airframe all over the world—to Britain, Greece, Israel, and Italy. It's a great machine!

—LTC Rick Rife, U.S. Army

Parked just aft of the island on the U.S.S. *Lincoln* are two SH-3 Sea Kings. Since space on a carrier deck is limited, the rotor blades and tail-rotor pylons on these helicopters are designed to be folded. Each of the rotor blades has been tied down, and both aircraft have been securely chained to the deck to keep them from moving as the ship rolls.

T58-GE-8 engines that spin a sixty-two-foot (18.9m) -diameter, five-bladed single main rotor. Later versions were upgraded to 1,400-horsepower General Electric T58-GE-8R engines. Its boat-hull fuselage is fifty-four feet, nine inches (16.7m) long and large enough inside for crew to stand upright. Maximum takeoff weight is 18,626 pounds (8,456kg) and maximum speed is 166 miles per hour (267kph). The H-3's boat-hull design, featuring two outrigger sponsons, allows for water landings. In heavier seas, the H-3 remains stable with the aid of the main rotor. Designed for shipboard storage, both the main and tail rotors fold.

For its ASW role, the Sea King was outfitted with a full complement of the latest electronic sub-hunting gear of the day, including: dipping sonar—a sonar unit that can be lowered from the hovering helicopter into the water for active (ping and listen) and passive (listen only) underwater search—and a MAD (magnetic anomaly detector) unit mounted in the starboard sponson, to detect the minute changes made by a submerged submarine to the Earth's magnetic field. The H-3's port sponson carried active and passive sonobuoys, or floating sonar transmitters that can be dropped into the water from the helicopter. (Active sonobuoys ping and listen, while passive sonobuoys listen only.) Also housed in the port sponson were smoke markers: dropped on the surface of the water, they mark and track the path of a submerged submarine. The Sea King's offensive weapons included the Mark 44 and Mark 48 torpedoes.

The H-3 was adapted for search and rescue by the U.S. Air Force. The Sea King was also used extensively by the U.S. Coast Guard for search and rescue. The U.S. Marine Corps helicopter detachment assigned to transport the President of the United States also flew Sea Kings. Sikorsky sold Sea Kings to the Canadian Air Force, to the Brazilian Navy, and to the Spanish Navy. Sea Kings were also built under license by Agusta of Italy, Mitsubishi of Japan, and Westland of Great Britain.

Desert Shield and Desert Storm saw these venerable workhorses logging more than 5,000 hours in combat SAR (search-and-rescue) missions, interdiction operations, logistics

ROTOR TALES—TRUE STORIES FROM THE SKY

Heroic Coast Guard Air Rescue During a Storm

At the time of this rescue, I was stationed at the Coast Guard Air Station in Clearwater, Florida. In Florida, you always have severe weather—tropical storms, hurricanes, and convective activity that rolls in every afternoon. It makes for some pretty demanding flying at times. We usually flew about 450 search-and-rescue cases each year from the Clearwater Air Station.

One of the most demanding SAR cases I flew took place in March of 1993. We had a big storm that kicked up out of nowhere. Since it wasn't hurricane season, it caught a lot of people off guard, including many vessels at sea in the area. In Florida they nicknamed it "The Storm of the Century." It originated south of Florida and moved up the entire eastern seaboard, wreaking havoc all the way.

We had twelve Sikorsky H-3 Sea Kings at the time. Some were assigned elsewhere or were down for maintenance. That night there were about six H-3s that were continuously gassed up, flying back and forth on missions with fresh crews. Our crew that night consisted of Tom Maine, our pilot; Russ Jones, the flight mechanic; Dan Edwards, our rescue swimmer; and me, as copilot.

We were sent to respond to an ELT [emergency locator transmitter]. Nearly all marine vessels carry ELTs, transmitters that we can home in on from the aircraft. A Falcon jet [an HU-25] out of Miami was on the scene in the Gulf of Mexico; its crew had located the ELT and reported seeing some lights in the water.

We took off right before dark, and temperatures were down in the cool sixties [about 18°C]. We were wearing our survival suits and insulated flight suits. The storm had produced consistent twenty-five-foot [7.6m] to thirty-foot [9m] waves, which are just tremendous for the Gulf of Mexico. The winds were at thirty to forty knots [35 mph to 46 mph (56kph to 74kph)] with occasional gusts.

It didn't take long to get there because of some strong tailwinds. We were probably making 180 knots [207 mph (333kph)] flying at an indicated airspeed of 120 [138 mph (222kph)]. We had a low ceiling and were flying at an altitude of about 500 feet [152m]. We overflew the ELT at 300 feet [91m] and immediately spotted a few people in the water. They were wearing some type of flotation device equipped with strobe lights. The vessel that sank was a Honduran freighter called the *Fantastico*. There were about ten people on board, but we could only see a few at the time.

We have some rescue maneuvers that are unique to the Coast Guard. We call them "patches and matches." A PATCH is a Precision Approach to a Coupled Hover; a MATCH is a Manual Approach to a Coupled Hover. We shoot these approaches at night with no other visual references to the horizon or to the water. It's extremely demanding flying—and we do these all the time.

We got down to a hover at fifty feet [15m] and stabilized into the wind. One thing we noted right away was that it wasn't taking much power to hover—we were only at about seventy percent power. The more wind you have coming across the rotors, the less power you need from the aircraft to hover. The airspeed indicator, which usually indicates zero in a hover, now was indicating anywhere from twenty-five knots [29 mph (46kph)] to forty-five knots [52 mph (83kph)].

Dan, our rescue swimmer, was already in the door with his gear on. We did a sling deployment to lower Dan down to the water and then backed off. Dan had to swim over to the first PIW [person in the water], and it took him quite a while to get there, mainly because of the waves and the winds.

Our standard procedure is to deploy the swimmer with the survivor positioned at about two o'clock, just outside the rotor wash. If you get a survivor underneath the rotor wash and he's close to losing consciousness, he can drown. It took Dan a long time to swim over to the first survivor because of the high seas. Once he got there, he signaled for a basket recovery. It was very difficult to maintain a steady hover because of the waves, winds, and lack of visual references. Although we had hover lights on the belly of the aircraft, our nose light was inoperable, and this hampered us a bit.

We went in for the first hoist. At this point, the flight mech gave us conning directions to pick up the survivor. Normally he'll say, "Forward in, right ten, forward in, right five, hold, basket's near the survivor, survivor's approaching the basket, survivor's in the basket, basket's off the water, basket's approaching the cabin"; that's a real standard hoist. The commands you normally give when you're over the survivor are "Hold, hold, easy left, easy right"; very smooth, small corrections.

That night, the smallest correction we got was "left thirty, right thirty" because we were being tossed about by the

he was in some kind of distress—we decided to get him next. Same evolution. We deployed Dan, he swam over to the raft, grabbed the guy, and took him off the raft. At this point, the raft blew away immediately. It took at least ten minutes to do a basket recovery of this survivor. Then we had to do a basket recovery of Dan. By now, Dan was completely exhausted, and another deployment was out of the question. In addition, we we're getting close to our "bingo fuel," so we had to start thinking about heading back to get gas.

We gave the inbound H-3 the position and heard that a C-130 was overhead dropping rafts to the survivors. As we departed, I specifically remember seeing two, maybe three, survivors floating down in the water with their PFDs [personal flotation devices] and lights in that green field of view through my NVGs [night-vision goggles]. There were only two survivors rescued from the *Fantastico* that night, and those were the two we got.

Petty Officer Dan Edwards was given the Distinguished Flying Cross. The DFC, awarded for heroism or extraordinary achievement in aerial flight, is one of the most prestigious medals anyone in the service of our country can be awarded. Pilot Tom Maine was awarded the Air Medal for meritorious achievement while participating in aerial flight. Petty Officer Russ Jones and I were both awarded the Coast Guard Commendation Medal for meritorious service resulting in outstanding achievement.

—LT Tim Tobiasz, U.S. Coast Guard

U.S. Coast Guard helicopter pilot Lieutenant Tim Tobiasz has made the transition from the H-3 Sea King to the Coast Guard's newest rescue helicopter, the HH-60 Jayhawk.

winds. The basket would get near the survivor and a wave would crest underneath the helo. The flight mechanic would think that the wave was going to hit the bottom of the aircraft, even though we were maintaining a thirty-to-thirty-five-foot [9m to 10.7m] hover. The waves were approaching the aircraft and we could see them rolling underneath. The basket would hit the top of the wave and be tossed back violently. The flight mechanic perceived that we were backing down. It was more or less a visual illusion when he was looking down. In addition, the object you're trying to pluck out of the water is also being tossed about by the waves. You may be in a stable hover, getting ready to pick up, then all of a sudden a wave washes the survivor thirty feet [9m] behind and away. It took a long time to recover the first survivor.

We finally got the survivor onboard the aircraft and then we had to recover Dan. Normally, Dan would just swim to the next survivor and we'd pick him up. But in this case, the next survivor was probably 100 yards [91m] away, and there was no way our rescue swimmer could swim 100 yards [91m] through thirty-foot [9m] seas and have the strength to rescue the next survivor. Besides, by this time it was so dark that Dan couldn't even see him. We sent the basket down for Dan and it took five to ten minutes just to get him back in.

We started hovering forward to find some more lights, and the first thing we came upon was a small orange raft with one guy lying down in it. We decided to move on to the next guy because he looked like he'd be okay in the raft. But as we hovered over him, he looked like

support, and mine location. Sea Kings were responsible for the location of more than thirty mines during the conflict. Fleet Sea Kings have been replaced by Sikorsky H-60 Seahawks for both plane guard and ASW missions. The Sea King is still proudly serving the U.S. Navy (albeit in small numbers) and is scheduled to do so until 2003.

★ CH-53 SEA STALLION AND CH-53E ★ SUPER STALLION

The CH-53 Sea Stallion first flew in 1964. It was a development of Sikorsky's successful Skycrane helicopter designed to meet the U.S. Marine Corps' need for a heavy-lift helicopter. The U.S. Marine Corps wanted it to transport supplies, equipment, and personnel from ship to shore during amphibious assault operations. The Sea Stallion would also be used as a transport for other airlift purposes. A rear ramp facilitates the loading or unloading of cargo or troops. Up to 8,000 pounds (3,632kg) can be carried externally in nets or slings. Internally, the Sea Stallion can transport thirty-seven battle-ready marines or be configured to carry twenty-four litters, if used for emergency medical evacuation.

OPPOSITE: Although aging, the U.S. Navy's Sea King helicopters performed admirably during Desert Shield/Desert Storm. Operating from carriers, the Sea Kings logged more than five thousand hours of search-and-rescue missions, interdiction operations, logistics support, and mine location.

BELOW: The CH-53E has a seven-bladed rotor measuring seventy-nine feet (24m) in diameter. The Super Stallion is the largest U.S. helicopter, exceeded in size only by the massive Russian Mi-26 Halo.

BELOW: The large sponsons on the side of this U.S. Navy Super Stallion house the retracted main landing gear. Mounted on the front of the fuselage is an extendible probe used for air-to-air refueling.

OPPOSITE: This CH-53E Super Stallion is about to touch down on the island of Grenada. The Super Stallion can carry fifty-five combat troops on folding canvas seats along the bulkheads and in the center of the cargo area. This CH-53 is equipped with drop tanks mounted on the outside of each main-wheel sponson.

The Sea Stallion is powered by two General Electric T64-GE-416 engines, which produce a total of 5,700 horsepower. Cruise speed is 130 knots (150 mph [241kph]) with a range of 600 nautical miles (690 miles [1,112km]). The U.S. Marine Corps is in the final phases of retiring all of its Sea Stallions in favor of the CH-53E Super Stallion.

The U.S. Air Force is in the process of modifying its earlier CH-53 B and C models into MH-53J Pave Lows for its Special Operations Forces. These enhanced helicopters are equipped with nose-mounted FLIR, terrain-following and terrain-avoidance radar, an advanced electronic countermeasures system, titanium armor plating, mounts for .50-caliber and 7.62mm mini-guns, and a refueling probe. Also included as part of the modification package are more powerful engines.

Second only to the Russian Mi-26 Halo, the CH-53E Super Stallion is the world's largest production helicopter.

Prototypes first flew in 1974 as a development of the earlier CH-53 Sea Stallion. By 1975, Super Stallion production prototypes were being tested. The U.S. Marine Corps received the first of its Super Stallions in June 1981, and by the summer of 1983 they were operational with a squadron deployed in the Mediterranean.

The extremely powerful Super Stallion looks very similar to the Sea Stallion, with a few notable exceptions. The Super Stallion has larger side sponsons, an additional engine, a seven-bladed main rotor, and a canted vertical stabilizer. These modifications give the Super Stallion superior load-carrying capabilities.

The most noticeable difference between earlier versions of the CH-53 and the CH-53E Super Stallion is the enlarged side sponsons, which house the main gear when retracted. These large sponsons also provide flotation to stabilize the air-

craft when conducting surface water operations. Within the forward portion of each sponson is a self-sealing fuel tank with a capacity of 315 gallons (1.2kl). Total internal fuel capacity is 1,017 gallons (3.9kl). This can be increased considerably by adding external tanks that attach to the sponsons or by carrying additional internal tanks. Air-to-air refueling from a KC-130 is possible with the Super Stallion's refueling probe mounted on the lower right side of the nose.

A third engine was added to the Super Stallion just above and to the rear of the port engine. These three General Electric T64-GE-416 turboshaft engines each generate 4,380 shaft horsepower. The fully articulated main rotor is seventy-nine feet (24m) in diameter and has seven blades. Each of the blades has a titanium spar, a Nomex honeycomb core and a composite skin, and is pressurized to reveal cracks. The large main rotor head is made of steel and titanium and uses elastometric bearings. The Super Stallion's four-bladed aluminum tail rotor is twenty feet (6m) in diameter. It's mounted on a tail pylon that is canted twenty degrees to port. This angled pylon provides the aircraft with a small amount of lift from the tail rotor and extends the range of the center of gravity. The earlier versions of the CH-53 Sea Stallion had a vertical tail pylon. The Super Stallion's canted pylon is made of Kevlar composites and can be hydraulically folded to starboard. The main rotor blades can also be folded for shipboard storage.

The primary portion of the Super Stallion's watertight fuselage is constructed of aluminum, steel, and titanium. Kevlar was used extensively in the cockpit's construction. The airframe is designed to withstand crash loads of twenty Gs vertical and ten Gs lateral. The landing gear is fully retractable and features a fully castoring (that is, able to turn in any direction) nose wheel.

The Super Stallion's empty weight is 33,228 pounds (15,086kg) and its maximum takeoff weight is 69,750 pounds (31,667kg). The centrally located external hook can carry a single load of up to 36,000 pounds (16,344kg). The Super Stallion can carry fifty-five combat troops in folding canvas seats along the walls and center of the cabin, or 32,000 pounds

(14,528kg) of cargo. The Super Stallion is flown by a crew of three: pilot, copilot, and crew chief.

The Super Stallion's long range and air-to-air refueling capabilities were dramatically demonstrated in 1991, when two CH-53Es were launched from two amphibious ships. Their destination was the American Embassy in Mogadishu, Somalia—421 miles (677km) away. There they rescued U.S. citizens and foreign allies who were being threatened by Somali rebels who had overthrown the government.

In 1983, the U.S. Navy took delivery of its special minesweeping version of the Super Stallion. Designated the MH-53E, this special version has greater fuel capacity than the standard Super Stallion. Six of these minesweepers were deployed to the Persian Gulf during Desert Shield/Desert Storm. There they logged 3,000 hours while participating in an extensive minesweeping campaign in the Gulf waters. Minesweeping is accomplished by towing a hydrofoil mine vehicle in the water by means of a long cable.

OPPOSITE: During the Gulf War, the MH-53E Super Stallions were used for minesweeping. Here, two Super Stallions pass by the *Idemitsu Maru*, a Japanese supertanker.

ABOVE: With a lifting capability of 36,000 pounds (16,344kg), this U.S. Marine Corps Super Stallion can transport a howitzer with ease.

★ SIKORSKY H-60 ★

(Black Hawk—U.S. Army; Pave Hawk—U.S. Air Force; White Hawk—U.S. Marine Corps; Seahawk—U.S. Navy; Jayhawk—U.S. Coast Guard)

The U.S. Army had determined in the early 1970s that the Huey would no longer meet its needs as a utility helicopter. The Army needed a new helicopter to carry out a variety of roles well into the next century. A proposal was developed for the new helicopter program, called Utility Tactical Transport Aircraft System. Sikorsky and Boeing Vertol both were selected in 1972 to build prototypes. Following testing, Sikorsky's design was selected and production of the Black Hawk began in 1977. The U.S. Army took delivery of its first UH-60A in 1978. Since then, the design has been adapted for use by all other branches of service, each with its own special requirements and variations of the Hawk name.

The H-60 is a conventionally designed helicopter with a fifty-three-foot, eight-inch (16m) -diameter single main rotor. Its eleven-foot (3.4m) -diameter tail rotor is mounted at the end of the tail boom above the horizontal stabilizer (commonly called a stabilator). The tail rotor is tilted to port to produce a small amount of lift as well as torque thrust. The H-60 is powered by twin General Electric 1700-GE-401 turboshaft engines (3,380 shaft horsepower) driven through a single transmission. The overall length is fifty feet (15m) and the height is sixteen feet, ten inches (5m). Its weight empty is 13,448 pounds (6,105kg), and fully loaded it scales out at 21,884 pounds (9,935kg). It can carry an internal payload of 2,640 pounds (1,199kg) or an external load of up to 9,000 pounds (4,086kg). The H-60's maximum speed is 169 miles per hour (272kph), with a range of 319 nautical miles (367.2 miles [591km]). That range can be extended considerably with the use of auxiliary fuel tanks. The H-60 can be transported longer

The MH-60G Pave Hawk is the U.S. Air Force version of the Sikorsky H-60. The Pave Hawk is used for special operations and combat search and rescue. All Pave Hawks are equipped with a hoist, a refueling probe, and .50-caliber machine guns.

distances by air cargo. A C-130 transport plane can carry one, a C-141 can carry two, and a C-5 can carry six H-60s.

An important design criterion was a crashworthy fuel system. To protect the fuel system, passengers, and internal components, the fuselage was built strong enough to survive hits from an AK-47 or any other .30-caliber weapon. The main rotor is strong enough to withstand a volley of .50-caliber gunfire. Other critical systems are either redundant or armor-plated. Additionally, the pilot's and copilot's seats are armor-plated. To further protect the crew, the H-60's airframe was

designed to crush progressively in the event of an accident. The crew's seats were also designed to absorb a hard landing or crash landing.

The H-60 is flown by a crew of three: pilot, copilot, and crew chief. In its Army Black Hawk configuration, the H-60 can transport an eleven-man infantry squad. Compared to the Huey, the Black Hawk can go farther, faster, and carry a bigger payload. A testament to the success of the machine's design, the U.S. Army currently has more than 1,500 Black Hawks in its inventory.

The U.S. Air Force version of the H-60 is designated MH-60G Pave Hawk. In the early 1980s the Air Force bought ninety-two UH-60A Black Hawk helicopters in standard army configuration. These Black Hawks were purchased to remedy a shortage in the Air Force's rescue helicopter inventory. Subsequently, Sikorsky Support Services of Troy, Alabama, began converting these UH-60As to the MH-60G Pave Hawk configuration. The conversion consists of the addition of an aerial refueling probe, an auxiliary fuel tank, and a fuel management panel. Additional avionics will consist of Doppler/INS, an electronic map display, TACAN (tactical air navigation), a lightweight weather/ground-mapping radar, secure HF (high-frequency radios) and Satcom, and .50-caliber machine guns. The updated avionics allow Pave Hawks to fly daytime or nighttime low-level missions in marginal weather. Ten Pave Hawks are in use with Special Operations units and the balance are assigned to combat rescue squadrons in active-duty, Reserve, and Air National Guard units.

The U.S. Navy flies the Seahawk (SH-60B) variant of the H-60, also known as the Light Airborne Multipurpose System (LAMPS) Mk III helicopter. The Seahawk is deployed on *Ticonderoga*-class cruisers, *Spruance*- and *Kidd*-class destroyers, and *Perry*-class frigates. These LAMPS helos provide all-weather capability for detection, classification, localization, and interdiction of ships and submarines. The Seahawk's secondary missions include search and rescue, medical evacuation, vertical replenishment, fleet support, and communications relay.

The U.S. Navy formed its first Seahawk squadron in 1984. Since then, the Seahawk has been upgraded regularly and has enjoyed a great deal of success in every mission to which it has been assigned. The SH-60F is a modified version that has replaced the aging Sikorsky Sea King as the carrier-based ASW helicopter. Its role is to protect the inner zone of the carrier battle group from submarine attacks. The HH-60H is another version of the Seahawk that has been modified for combat search and rescue. The Navy is now in the process of modifying 170 of the original B versions and 18 of the F models into

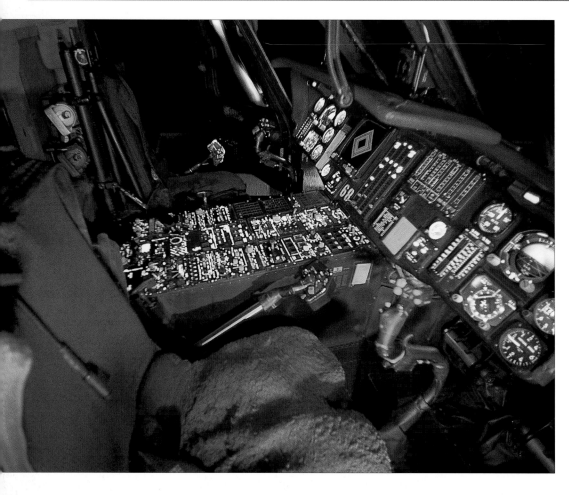

PREVIOUS PAGE: Replacing the H-3 Sea King in an ASW (anti-submarine warfare) role is the SH-60F Seahawk. Operating from aircraft carriers, it protects the inner zone of the carrier battle group from enemy submarine attacks.

ABOVE: The cockpit of the H-60 Blackhawk is laid out efficiently. The console splitting the two comfortable seats contains the communications gear. There is a set of flight instruments directly in front of each seat.

a new variant, the SH-60R. The new SH-60R configuration incorporates new sonar, upgraded electronic support measures, and integrated self-protection systems. The remanufacturing is scheduled to start in 1999 and be completed in 2007. These modifications will extend the service life of the airframe from 10,000 to 20,000 hours. Future plans call for arming the Seahawks with Hellfire and Penguin missiles.

The U.S. Coast Guard version of the H-60 is very similar to the Navy's SH-60F version. The HH-60J Jayhawk replaced the HH-3 Pelican as the Coast Guard's medium-range recovery helicopter. Since it was first delivered to the Coast Guard in 1990, the Jayhawk has proved itself by performing rescues in snowstorms and hurricanes. With three external 120-gallon (454l) fuel tanks, the Jayhawk has a range of 300 nautical miles (345 miles [555km]). It's typically flown with a crew of four: pilot, copilot, crew chief, and rescue swimmer. The Jayhawk has enough internal room to carry six survivors in addition to the crew. The Coast Guard's independent offshore

work has been enhanced by the Jayhawk's GPS (global positioning system) navigation array and coupled-Doppler hover capability. Other roles for the Coast Guard's H-60s include law enforcement, drug interdiction, logistics, aids to navigation, environmental protection, and tracking smugglers.

The U.S. Marine Corps adapted its version of the H-60 as an executive transport for the White House. Appropriately, it's named the White Hawk. It has replaced the aging Sea King helicopters in the U.S. Marine's HMX-1 squadron based at Quantico, Virginia. The version the marines fly for their important missions is designated the VH-60N. The White Hawk features a more durable gearbox, increased fuel capacity, VIP interior, and additional sound-proofing.

The Sikorsky H-60 has picked up where the Huey left off as a very flexible platform for a variety of missions. It has been purchased by dozens of nations for a variety of military roles. The H-60 should be flying long into the twenty-first century, adapted to roles not yet imagined.

★ RAH-66 COMANCHE ★

The Boeing/Sikorsky RAH-66 Comanche is the foundation of the U.S. Army's Aviation Modernization plan. It's the army's newest air cavalry helicopter. The Comanche's multimission capabilities include armed reconnaissance, attack, and air combat. It's designed to replace the Army's current fleet of AH-1, OH-6, and OH-58 helicopters. Key features of the new design include improved sensors, increased maneuverability, agility, speed, and stealth.

The Comanche is designed around a lightweight, all-composite airframe. Its twin T-801 turboshaft engines each

Following a rescue, a U.S. Coast Guard rescue swimmer is the last one hoisted back up into the HH-60 Jayhawk. During the hoisting operation, the pilot must keep a steady hover to prevent the person being hoisted from swinging out of control.

BELOW: The RAH-66 Comanche is the U.S. Army's newest attack helicopter, scheduled to be in service by 2006. Its primary mission will be armed reconnaissance and attack.

OPPOSITE: The Comanche's fuselage (foreground) incorporates the latest in stealth technology. It has an internal weapons bay. Stub wings can be added for an expanded ordnance load. Flying in the background is an AH-64 Apache Longbow.

develop 1,563 horsepower and drive a five-bladed main rotor thirty-nine feet (11.9m) in diameter. The composite, hingeless rotor hub eliminates many components and increases reliability. The large tail rotor is a ducted design and, like the main rotor, is designed to produce a low acoustical signature. The main rotor can be folded, making the Comanche easily delivered by U.S. Air Force transport aircraft.

The fuselage was designed using the latest Computer Aided Design tools and produces a low radar signature. The Comanche was built with maintainability designed in: numerous panels on the fuselage allow easy access to electronic and mechanical components that can be replaced on the flight line, as well as to connectors for advanced diagnostic systems. The Comanche's weapons bay doors double as work platforms, so that maintenance mechanics can work without ladders or stands. Other design features include a low heat signature—made possible by engine exhaust ducts—and retractable landing gear.

The Comanche's two crewmen sit in tandem in a sealed, pressurized cockpit with the pilot in the front seat and the co-pilot in the rear. The crew's helmet displays superimpose integrated flight and target information so the crew can fly and fight their mission heads-up, with their vision on the terrain. The Comanche has a highly refined version of the digital map system currently in place on the F-117 Stealth fighter. This system can simultaneously display the terrain, friendly forces, known enemy positions, and preplanned mission routes. Comanche's cruise speed is 165 knots (190 mph [306kph]), with a maximum range of 1,260 nautical miles (1,450 miles [2,334km]). The Comanche carries 302 gallons (1.1kl) of fuel internally; external tanks can be added for an additional 900 gallons (3.4kl).

On the nose of the Comanche is the long-range infrared/TV targeting sensor and the infrared piloting sensor/low-visibility image intensifier. Mounted below those sensors is the chin-mounted 20mm turreted cannon. Unlike other attack helicopters, the Comanche has two internal weapons bays. These bays can hold a variety of missiles, including Hellfire, Stinger, 2.75-inch rockets, TOW missiles, and the new Longbow Hellfire. When these bays are closed, the radar signature and aerodynamic drag are dramatically reduced. These bays can be opened and a weapon fired within three seconds. Stub wings with external pylons can be added to increase the Comanche's weapons load.

The Comanche program has completed its concept exploration and initial demonstration phase. The prototype phase was initiated, and on April 12, 1991, a contract was awarded to the Boeing/Sikorsky team. In March 1995, the U.S. Secretary of Defense approved a program that would provide two flyable prototypes and six additional aircraft for evaluation. The Comanche's first flight was on January 4, 1996. The testing and evaluation phase will last through 2003. The Comanche is expected to be operational in 2006.

RUSSIAN MILITARY HELICOPTERS

The first notable Russian helicopter designer was Mikhail Mil, often called the Sikorsky of Russian helicopter design. His first successful helicopter was the Mi-1 (NATO code name: Hare), which had its maiden flight in 1950. The Mi-1 had a 550-horsepower engine and a four-bladed rotor with a span of forty-five feet, eleven inches (14m). In 1952, Mil produced the Mi-4 as a troop carrier; it looked very like the American Sikorsky S-55, which had first flown two years earlier. The Mi-4 was larger than the S-55, capable of carrying fourteen combat troops or twenty passengers in a civilian configuration. In its era, the Mi-4 set many helicopter records and had a long service life.

In 1957, Mil's design bureau built the largest helicopter in the world, the Mi-6, which set the world record by lifting a 26,964-pound (12,242kg) load. The Mi-6 was also very aerodynamic, setting a speed record of 199.4 miles per hour (321kph). The Mi-6 was the precursor of the larger Mi-26, currently the world's largest helicopter. The Mil Design Bureau also developed the very successful Mi-24 Hind and the Mi-28 Havoc.

Unconventional would be one way to describe the helicopters designed by Nikolai Kamov, an early pioneer of Russian helicopter design. In 1947, his Ka-8 flew for the first time. It was a single-seat ultra-light that featured a coaxial main rotor. Kamov refined that design into the Ka-10, which was used by the Russian Navy, and perfected coaxial rotor configurations, a type of design shunned by Western designers. Today, the Russian Ka-27 Helix and Ka-50 Hokum are two excellent examples of coaxial rotor technology. The Ka-50 also features an ejection seat for the pilot.

★ MI-24, 25, AND 35 HIND ★

The Soviet Mi-24 (NATO code name: Hind) is a twin-turbine helicopter gunship with transport capability. Its development at the Mil Design Bureau began in the late 1960s as a fire support platform able to transport armed ground soldiers. The Hind's first flight was in September 1969, but it was unknown in the West until 1972. In 1974, the first Hind photograph surfaced as a result of a Soviet deployment of two Hind squadrons to East Germany. The conversion to the gunship configuration took place in the mid-1970s and was first spotted in 1977.

Of the 2,500 Hinds produced, 800 are in service with the Russian Army. Other countries using the Hind include Afghanistan, Angola, Croatia, Cuba, India, Iraq, North Korea, Libya, Peru, and Vietnam.

The Hind is a conventionally designed attack helicopter with stepped tandem seating for the rear-seated pilot and forward-seated weapons officer. Both sit in armored seats in cockpits separated by an antifragment shield. A separate canopy for each officer has an optically flat, bulletproof front windscreen. The forward-seated weapons operator has a set of flight con-

trols, but the foot pedals are retractable. There is a small passageway between the main cabin and the pilot's cockpit.

For a gunship, the Hind is unusually wide (almost six feet [1.8m]), due to its troop transportation requirements. The Hind can carry four stretchers or eight soldiers in folding jump seats. Its overall length is fifty-seven feet, five inches (17.5m), with a height of thirteen feet (4m). The fuselage is an all-metal, semi-monocoque design with 5mm-thick hardened steel side armor on the front fuselage. The Hind's stub wings are metal and have no moveable surfaces. These short wings provide 25 percent of the lift at cruising speed. At the end of the tail boom is a variable-pitch horizontal stabilizer.

The five-bladed rotor is fifty-six feet, nine inches (17.3m) in diameter. Each rotor blade has a honeycomb core with an aluminum spar and skin. The blades are pressurized with nitrogen to facilitate crack detection. The tail rotor is an aluminum alloy, three-bladed design.

Mounted above the cabin are two Klimov TV3-117MT turboshaft engines, each producing 1,923 shaft horsepower. They drive rearward through a gearbox to the main rotor shaft. Both engines are surrounded with 5mm-thick armor plating and have intake filters to shield against ingesting damaging objects and dust. The exhaust has mixer boxes that blend outside air with exhaust fumes to reduce the engine's infrared signature. The Hind's main fuel tank is located behind the cabin, and there are additional tanks to the rear of the gearbox. This gives the Hind an internal capacity of 3,307 pounds (1,501kg) of fuel. This can be supplemented by an additional cabin-mounted tank and external tanks mounted on the wing pylons.

The Hind can carry a formidable assortment of armament. Under the nose is a chin-mounted 12.7mm Gatling-type gun. The magazine for this machine gun carries 1,470 rounds. Its field of fire is sixty degrees to each side, sixty degrees down, and twenty degrees up. The reflector sight is mounted in the forward cockpit and slaved to the undernose sighting system. The wing pylons can be configured to carry a wide variety of weapons, including antitank missiles, 57mm

The boom extending out from the front of the lower cockpit is a low-speed air data sensor. It feeds precise data changes on the aircraft's airspeed, altitude, and side forces to the weapons-aiming computer. Each cockpit has a flat, bulletproof glass windscreen.

rockets, 130mm rockets, 240mm rockets, a variety of machine guns, grenade launchers, up to 3,000 pounds (1,362kg) of conventional bombs, mine dispensers, or night flares. Air-to-air missiles have been fired experimentally from these pylons. Machine guns can also be mounted in the cabin windows. The Hind can carry additional stores in the cabin to reload the pylons in the field.

Several versions of the basic Mi-24 Hind have been manufactured for specific customers or with slightly different standard armament configurations. The Mi-24K was built for reconnaissance and artillery fire correction. The Mi-24PS was a special version built for the Russian Ministry of Internal Affairs and was displayed at the 1995 Moscow Air Show. It featured an undernose FLIR ball, port-side searchlight, and a loudspeaker pack. The Mi-25 is an export version of the Mi-24D that has been sold to Afghanistan, Cuba, and India.

One of the most unusual Hind configurations is the Mi-24R. It was at the site of the Chernobyl nuclear powerplant following the accident in April 1986. This R variant was devoid of undernose electro-optical and RF missile guidance pods. Replacing the wing weapon mounts were clutching-hand mechanisms on lengthened pylons. These mechanisms were used to gather soil samples on flights into the accident area. These samples were retrieved for nuclear, biological, and chemical analysis. During flight into the area, air samples were drawn in and the results data-linked to the ground. The crew of four all wore nuclear/biological/chemical (NBC) suits.

The most recent version of the Hind is the Mi-35M. This model has been upgraded to meet the latest night-capable requirements of the Russian Army. The Mi-35 has been fitted with more powerful Klimov TV3-117VMA engines. The main and tail rotors are the same as those used on the Mi-28 Havoc. The Mi-35 is lighter by virtue of composite rotor blades, a titanium head, new avionics, shortened stub wings, and nonretractable landing gear. A FLIR pod is mounted on the port side of the forward fuselage, providing night vision for target acquisition and identification, missile guidance, and gun aiming. The first Mi-35M was seen at the 1995 Paris Air Show.

The Russian Ka-27 (NATO code name: Helix) was first spotted by Western observers in 1981 on the rear deck of a Russian antisubmarine guided-missile destroyer. The civilian version, designated Ka-32, was also first seen by Western eyes in 1981. The Helix design was born out of its predecessor, the Ka-25 Hormone. The Helix has a pair of coaxial counter-rotating, three-bladed rotors. On both the military and civilian versions of the Helix, all blades can be folded toward the rear. All Russian ship-based helicopters share the three-bladed rotor design. Both rotors are fifty-two feet, two inches (15.9m) in diameter and are made of composite material.

The coaxial counter-rotating rotor design of the Helix eliminates the need for a tail rotor. But this type of design typ-

ABOVE: These Russian pilots and weapons system officers fly the Hind attack helicopter. They have trained at the Saratov Training Center in the former Central Soviet Asia.

RIGHT: The Hind's front cockpit is for the weapons systems officer. The optical unit on the far bulkhead is a missile control sight.

The Helix has fulfilled a series of missions since it first entered the Russian service. It was initially deployed with the Russian Navy for ASW missions. Later versions of the Helix have been used as assault transports and as electronic warfare platforms.

ically produces vibrations that reduce aircraft life and increase the need for maintenance. According to the Kamov Design Bureau, the Helix's main rotor system has been redesigned to reduce vibration. Kamov attached the main rotor shaft with straps, and the lower rotor uses adjustable weights.

In its ASW role, the Helix has an autopilot that allows automated approach and hover. The Helix also has a system that maintains constant rotor thrust during turns.

Power for the Helix comes from a pair of Klimov TV3-117BK engines, which produce a total of 4,340 shaft horsepower. These are the same engines that power the Mi-24 Hind. With this surplus of power, single-engine flight is possible. The Helix has a maximum speed of 168 miles per hour (270kph) and a range of more than 100 miles (161km).

The Helix has a large cargo capacity. Internally it can carry close to 9,000 pounds (4,086kg) of payload. If the load is slung on a hook beneath the fuselage, the Helix can carry 11,000 pounds (4,994kg). In its troop-carrying configuration, the Helix can carry sixteen soldiers plus a crew of three. Access to the internal cargo area is through a large sliding door on the left side. This large cargo-carrying capability proved vital for the civilian version, which was used to ferry construction equipment to remote locations. Civilian versions are also used for search-and-rescue as well as fire fighting.

Kamov built the Helix in four basic configurations. The Russian Navy uses the A, B, and D models. The A version is used for its ship-based ASW operations. The B model is deployed on amphibious assault ships and is used as a troop transport. The D is based on *Kiev*-class aircraft carriers, where it's used as a plane guard and in a search-and-rescue role. The Helix C model is the civilian version of this helicopter; it is also known by the designation Ka-32.

TOP: The Kamov Helix does not have a tail rotor, because its design features twin counterrotating main rotors to counteract torque. Because of inherent vibration problems, this configuration has been shunned by Western designers. Powering the Helix are the same Klimov engines used on the Hind.

BOTTOM: The highly adaptable Russian Helix is flown by both the navy and army. The navy versions are used as plane guards, for ASW, and search-and-rescue. Army versions of the Helix are used as troop transports (shown here) and can be armed for a light attack role. A civilian and export version of the Helix is designated the Ka-32.

★ MIL MI-28 HAVOC ★

The design stage of the Mi-28 Havoc started in 1980. On November 10, 1982, the first of four prototypes flew. At the 1994 Asian Aerospace show, one of these prototypes was demonstrated. The Russian Army announced in 1994 its requirement that the Havoc have night and all-weather flight characteristics. At the 1995 Moscow Air Show, the first of the modified prototypes with expanded capabilities was shown. It was designated the Mi-28N.

The Mi-28N Havoc is powered by two Klimov TV3-117VM turboshaft engines, each rated at 2,465 shaft horsepower. These engines are mounted in pods above each wing root. Deflectors are mounted in front of the intakes to prevent foreign objects and dust from entering the engines. Ducts cool and deflect the engine's exhaust stream downward. Some of the prototypes have had upswept exhaust ducts. An Ivchenko APU is located in the rear of the main pylon structure. It supplies compressed air for starting the main engine and also to

drive a small turbine for maintenance tests and inspections on the ground.

The Havoc's five-bladed main rotor is 105 feet (32m) in diameter. The blades are constructed of composites with a Nomex-like honeycomb core. The tips are swept back and a titanium strip covers the leading edge. The main rotor head is machined titanium with an elastomeric bearing, which needs no lubrication. The tail rotor is a combination of two independent two-bladed rotors on the same shaft. The blades are set in a 35- and 145-degree spacing pattern, in what has been described as a "scissors" configuration.

Above the main rotor is a 360-degree scan millimeter wave radar. A FLIR ball is mounted beneath the missile-guidance nose radome, which houses the radar antennae, and above the optical/laser sensors. The optical weapons sight and laser range sensors are turret-mounted and can swing 110 degrees to each side.

The Havoc's multiple internal fuel tanks hold 2,947 pounds (1,338kg) of fuel. They are self-sealing, wrapped in a

In flight, the Russian Mi-28 Havoc resembles the U.S. Army's Apache. Like the Apache, the Havoc was designed as an attack helicopter. It is powered by two Klimov TV3-117VM turboshaft engines, each developing 2,465 shaft horsepower. The Havoc has a service ceiling of 19,025 feet (5800m) and a maximum cruise speed of 145 knots (167mph/267kph).

composite skin. These tanks are impervious to fire or explosion if hit by bullets or shell fragments. All of the Havoc's major aircraft systems are redundant, and all vital systems are shielded with titanium armor. The Havoc is designed so that a single hit cannot knock out both engines.

The Havoc's pilot sits in the rear cockpit, and the navigator/gunner sits in the front. Both cockpits are pressurized and air conditioned. Crew survivability was emphasized in the design of the Havoc. Surrounding the cockpits are titanium and ceramic armor. An armored panel separates the two cockpits. Each of the cockpit's flat plate-glass panels is bulletproof. Energy-absorbing seats and landing gear are designed to protect the crew in a crash. The crew's side-access doors are

hinged in the rear to open quickly and remain open in case of an emergency. Both Havoc crew members wear parachutes. If they are required to bail out, an emergency system jettisons the cockpit doors. Detonators remove the stub wings from the airframe, then door sill bladders inflate. These bladders are designed to deflect the crew members away from the main landing gear upon their exit from the cockpit, while the aircraft is still airborne.

A port-side door aft of the wing allows access to the avionics compartment. This access bay is large enough for an emergency rescue of two or three soldiers on the ground. This compartment would only be used in an emergency situation, as it lacks heating and proper ventilation.

Centered in the Havoc's cockpit instrument panel is a CRT (cathode ray tube) for the nose-mounted video camera. Both cockpits are surrounded with titanium and ceramic armor plating.

The Havoc has stub wings similar to those of all other attack helicopters. These swept-back wings are composed of an alloy structure with composite leading and trailing edges and no moveable surfaces. Under each stub wing are two pylons, each capable of carrying 1,000 pounds (454kg) of ordnance. A typical weapons load could consist of sixteen 9M114 Shturm radio-guided tube-launched antitank missiles and two pods of twenty 80mm C-8 rockets or 130mm C-13 rockets. These wing-mounted guided weapons are launched from the front cockpit. The unguided rockets can be launched from either cockpit.

Under the nose is a turret-mounted 30mm cannon with 250 rounds of ammunition. It has a maximum rate of fire of 900 rounds per minute and can be used for air-to-air or air-to-ground attacks (this particular gun is also used by Russian ground vehicles). The cannon's turret can sweep in a 110-degree side-to-side arc. It can also be aimed 40 degrees down or 13 degrees up. This cannon is directed and fired by the weapons officer in the front seat. If the gun is locked in its straight-ahead position, it can be fired by the pilot in the rear seat.

★ MI-26 HALO ★

The Mi-26 Halo is a twin-turbine heavy-lift helicopter. It is the world's largest production helicopter. The Halo's development started in the early 1970s. The designer's goal was to produce a helicopter with a load capacity twice that of any contemporary helicopter. The first Mi-26 Halo prototype flew in December 1977 and was first displayed at the Paris Air Show in 1981. In 1982, Russian squadrons received their first Halos, which were not fully operational until 1983. In 1986, India was the first country to purchase a Halo. Since then Halos have been sold to nearly twenty countries. The cost of a Halo is between $10 million and $12 million.

The Halo has the load-carrying capability of a domestic C-130 transport plane. Its cargo area, with the rear ramp closed, is thirty-nine feet, four inches (12m) long, and ten feet, six inches (3.2m) wide, with a minimum ceiling height of nine

feet, eight inches (2.9m). This cargo area can hold two combat vehicles weighing 22,000 pounds (9,988kg) each. The interior can be configured to seat eighty combat-equipped troops or sixty stretchers. The Halo is flown by a crew of four: pilot, copilot, flight engineer, and navigator. The flight deck and cabin are fully air conditioned, but only the flight deck is pressurized.

The Halo's landing gear is a noretractable tricycle-type with a steerable nose wheel. The main gear can be hydraulically adjusted to facilitate loading through the rear door. This adjustable feature is also used when landing on varied surfaces. Each of the main gears has a sensor to determine takeoff weight. This information is displayed at the flight engineer's station at liftoff. The Halo's retractable tail skid offers unrestricted accessibility to the rear cargo loading door. There is a hatch on the underside of the fuselage that opens to give

The Mi-28 Havoc's bulbous nose radome houses a radio used for missile guidance. Below the radome are the daylight weapons sight and the laser range designator. The 30mm gun below fires at a rate of 900 rounds per minute. The gunner/navigator controls the gun, which can be rotated 110 degrees to each side.

TOP: The Russian Mi-26 Halo is the largest helicopter in the world. It's used as a military transport, civilian transport, air tanker, and air crane. The Halo's cargo bay is similar in size to the cargo bay on a Lockheed C-130.

BOTTOM: The flight deck of the Russian Halo is as roomy as any large airliner. Up front, the pilot sits on the left side, with the copilot on his right. Behind the pilot is a station for the flight engineer, and to the flight engineer's right is the navigator's station.

access to a load sling. This sling is attached to an internal winch that's in-line with the main rotor shaft. Closed-circuit television cameras enable crew members to monitor the load beneath the aircraft.

The Halo was the first helicopter to successfully fly with an eight-blade main rotor. This rotor is 105 feet (32m) in diameter and is made of composites and aluminum alloys, with a leading edge made of titanium. The main rotor head and the tail rotor head are both made of titanium. The flight controls are hydraulically boosted with a redundant autopilot and stability-augmentation system. The enormous Halo is powered by two 10,000-shaft-horsepower ZMKB Progress D-136 turboshaft engines. Each engine bay is made of titanium for protection against fire.

Several variants of the Mi-26 Halo have been built. The Mi-26T is a civil transport version that is essentially the same as the military model. Included in the T designation are a firefighting version that's able to carry 1,980 gallons (7.5kl) of fire retardant, and a geological survey version that is used for towing seismic gear. The Mi-26P Halo is a transport version that can accommodate sixty-three passengers in airline-type seating. Amenities for the transport include a galley and a restroom. The Mi-26TZ is a tanker that can carry 3,710 gallons (14kl) of additional fuel. This fuel can be dispensed by four hoses to other aircraft, or by ten hoses to ground vehicles. The Mi-26MS is a full medical evacuation version. It houses an operating room, pre-op section, laboratory, restroom, scrub facilities, and food storage. The Mi-26TM is a flying crane. An under-fuselage gondola is large enough for the crane operator and one other person.

The latest and most powerful variant is the Mi-26M. All M-version Halos are equipped with two ZMKB Progress D-127 turboshaft engines. These engines each produce approximately 14,000 shaft horsepower. This additional power increases the maximum payload to 55,000 pounds (24,970kg). The additional power provided by these engines also allows maximum payload-carrying ability at high altitude and in warm weather, conditions that are generally detrimental to any helicopter's performance.

★ KAMOV KA-50 HOKUM ★

The first Western reports of a new Soviet close-support helicopter were made in mid-1984. Photographs of this new helicopter were first printed in a U.S. Department of Defense document, *Soviet Military Power*, published in 1989. The Ka-50 Hokum (also known as Werewolf) debuted at the Farnborough Air Show in 1992. What the attendees saw at that air show was the world's first single-seat combat helicopter. Even more amazing, the Hokum had an ejection seat for the pilot.

Design of the Hokum began at the Kamov Design Bureau in 1977. The Hokum's first flight was on July 27, 1982. Prior to its Western debut at the Farnborough Air Show, twelve pre-production models were built and tested against the Soviet Union's other attack helicopter, the Mi-28 Havoc. Testing of the Ka-50 Hokum continued through 1995.

The Ka-50 Hokum is designed for fast, low-flying, and close-range attacks. Its maximum speed in level flight is 193 miles per hour (310.5kph), and it can reach speeds of 217 miles per hour (349.2kph) in a shallow dive. It is supported on a pair of coaxial counterrotating rotors made of composite material. These forty-seven-foot, seven-inch (14.5m)-diameter rotors are widely separated along the vertical axis. The rotor's blades are semirigid and feature swept-back tips. The Hokum is powered by two Klimov TV3-117VM turboshaft engines, each producing 2,465 shaft horsepower. These engines are mounted above the wing roots and are fitted with intake dust filters and exhaust heat suppressors. Fuel is provided from internally mounted foam-filled tanks. Provisions are available to mount up to four external tanks.

Composite materials make up 35 percent of the Hokum's structure. Approximately 770 pounds (350kg) of armor protects the pilot and critical airframe components. The Hokum's double-walled cockpit protects the pilot from 23mm rounds fired from as close as 100 yards (91m). Much of the Ka-50's fuselage skin is formed by large hinged panels. These panels provide ground-level access to interior components. The Hokum has retractable tricycle landing gear. When retracted, the wheels are semiexposed.

The Russian Ka-50 Hokum is the world's first single-seat, close-support helicopter. It is heavily armored and features coaxial counterrotating three-bladed rotors. The Hokum has an ejection seat that allows the pilot to eject at any altitude.

Directly below the Ka-50's engines are two wings extending outboard at mid-fuselage. These wings can carry four underwing pods containing up to eighty S-8 80mm air-to-surface rockets. Or the wings can be configured with up to twelve Vikhr-M laser-guided air-to-surface missiles in tube launchers. These missiles are armor-piercing and have a range of up to six miles (9.7km). A load combination of both weapons is also possible. The wings can also be configured for up to 3,000 pounds (1,362kg) of other weapons, including gun pods, bombs, and other missile launchers. At the tips of these wings are additional pods, which contain a total of 128 chaff and flare cartridges.

Mounted under the starboard side of the Hokum's nose is a single-barrel 30mm cannon. It is fed from two fuselage-mounted magazines containing 280 rounds of ammunition. This gun can be aimed in a downward direction up to 30 degrees, and 5 degrees to each side. The pilot is equipped with a Mig-29-type helmet sight and heads-up display (HUD). With the target centered on the HUD, the pilot can push a button and lock the target into the digital autopilot.

The Hokum's pilot sits behind a large flat piece of bullet-proof glass; the Zyezda K-37 ejection seat was designed specifically for the Hokum for ejection at any altitude or airspeed. When the ejection process is initiated, the rotor blades are separated by means of an explosive device. The cockpit roof is also detonated. Finally, the pilot rides free of the aircraft on a large rocket. An automatically activated radio beacon is energized upon ejection. A life raft and survival kit are part of the ejection-seat system. If the pilot does not want to use the ejection seat, he has the option of rolling out the side door.

By design, the Ka-50 Hokum appears to be the world's premier air-combat helicopter. It carries the capabilities of a jet fighter in an agile helicopter airframe. Today, the Western countries have no counterpart to the Ka-50 Hokum.

POLICE HELICOPTERS

The first police air unit in the United States was established in New York City in 1929 with fixed-wing aircraft. In 1948, the New York City Aviation Unit became the first to introduce helicopters—Bell 47s—for police work. Over the years, police departments worldwide have established air units to support their officers on the street. Meticulous record keeping by the Airborne Law Enforcement Association (ALEA) continues to support the widely known advantages of improved response time, increased officer safety, and more effective surveillance and suppression of criminal activity.

The San Bernardino, California, Sheriff's Department has found it economical to buy surplus military helicopters and rebuild them for specific missions. This Twin-Huey has been outfitted for mountain rescue and has a hoist that stows in the rear cargo area when not in use.

The Los Angeles Police Department Air Support Division annually responds to more than 30,000 crime-in-progress calls each year, of which more than 6,000 might be air-assisted felony arrests. Often referred to as a "force multiplier," one airborne unit equates to five or more ground units. In addition, an aircraft is a powerful public relations tool. Citizens know that the police have made a commitment to their safety (and the criminals know it's not going to be easy to commit a crime) when there's a police helicopter buzzing around the neighborhood.

Some law enforcement agencies fly primarily government surplus aircraft purchased at a very low initial cost. The aircraft are rebuilt and maintained by the department's aircraft mechanics. Some units use federal surplus equipment to make having an air unit more affordable. Many departments with jurisdiction over large areas of uninhabited land have purchased surplus H-34 Choctaw and AH-1 Hueys to use as search-and-rescue aircraft.

A unique source of funding for a police air unit is the seized-asset account. Seized assets are properties taken from convicted criminals. These assets (automobiles, aircraft, boats, real estate, and cash) were in some way used by a criminal in the course of committing a crime, or were purchased with funds acquired illegally. Several police departments are currently flying helicopters and using specialized equipment thanks to this provision.

LAW ENFORCEMENT MISSIONS AND TRAINING

The missions of today's law enforcement helicopters vary among police air units depending on the needs of the community and the financial resources of the department. They include some or all of the following assignments: patrol (felony calls, silent alarms, rapes, robbery, murder, serious misdemeanors, lost or missing persons, vehicle pursuits, high-risk warrants), speed enforcement, surveillance (narcotics, gang activity, large groups, suspicious activity, roof checks, stolen vehicles), search-and-rescue (desert, mountain, coastline, river, delta, lake, canyon), medical evacuation, deployment of SWAT

21-08-96
0729:132

teams, special events, interagency assistance (Fire, EPA, DOJ), and assistance during natural disasters (earthquake, tornado, fire, flood).

The primary mission for rotary-wing air units within a law enforcement agency is to support fellow officers on the ground. A pilot and an observer (also a pilot) respond to calls that direct them to a crime in progress or to a designated location called in by a ground unit. The job of the pilot is to fly the aircraft and operate the radio. The observer's role is to communicate to ground units below, advising them of what's happening beyond their field of view.

During a high-speed pursuit, this could mean calling out the street names, the status of traffic along cross streets, whether the driver has abandoned the vehicle, and where the driver has gone. This kind of backup from above allows ground units to remain farther behind a fleeing suspect. Once the air unit has spotted a suspect, there is usually no getting away. Department liability is significantly reduced when vehicle pursuits are coordinated from an aerial platform.

With few exceptions, police air unit pilots are sworn officers with proven records as solid street cops who may have even paid for their own basic flight training. Each department seems to have different criteria for incoming prospective pilots. Some units require at least two years of road experience, a commercial license with instrument rating, and 300 flight

hours as pilot-in-command to test for placement on an eligibility list for future openings. In other units, officers must get an FAA Private Rotor Craft License to apply, with further training provided in-house. And there are a few law enforcement agencies with requirements so rigorous that only former military helicopter pilots with significant flight hours under their belts can meet them.

Ongoing training in police air units is part of normal operations. The Airborne Law Enforcement Association sponsors seminars for its members in flying tactics for law enforcement. The goal of this training is to increase productivity, safety, and standardization of police helicopter flight crews. Topics include mission planning, aerial search techniques, ground vehicle pursuit, ground-to-air communications, and the effective use of surveillance equipment. In addition, air units conduct their own regular training activities. Those with a rescue mission will drill on hoist operations, insertion and extraction of crew and patients, rappelling, and flight maneuvers such as the one-skid landing. Some air units (LAPD, San Bernardino

OPPOSITE: This police helo has a color screen that displays either a FLIR image or a video camera's view of the action being tracked. On the bulkhead below the screen is a pair of gyrostabilized binoculars.

LEFT: FLIR is a great tool for fighting crime from the air. It senses the heat an object gives off and displays it on an onboard monitor. In this infrared image, the hot engines of cars on the street below produce pronounced hot spots.

BELOW: The New York City Police Department was the first in the nation to have an air unit. This is a Bell JetRanger, one of the most popular helicopters in use by police.

Air ambulances have become indispensable. Here, a Bell LongRanger has landed on a suburban street to pick up an accident victim. The EMS team was on the scene early and called for the helicopter to provide quick transport to the trauma unit of a nearby hospital.

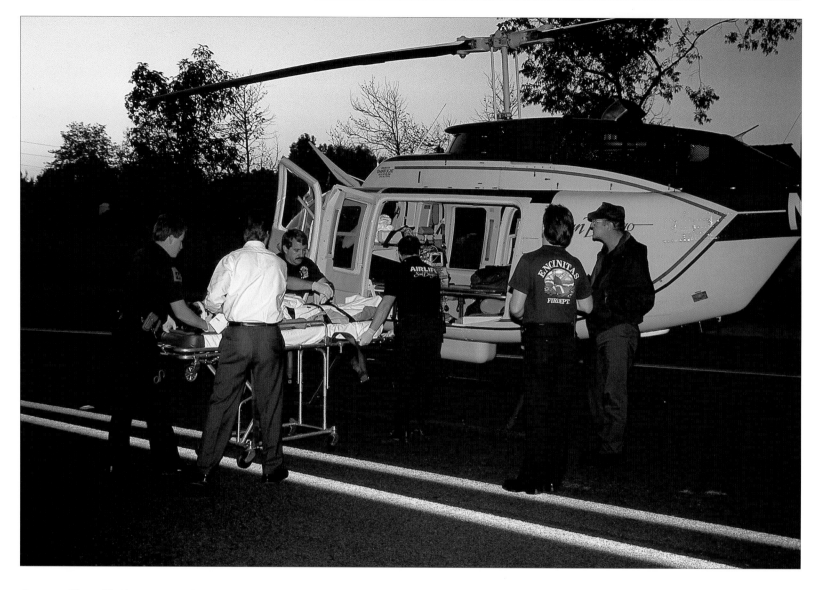

County Sheriff's Department) train and offer their expertise in live-fire operations. A dangerous and seldom-used tactical option, live-fire tactical training might include the insertion and extraction of sniper teams from rooftops.

The type of helicopter flown by a police air unit depends on its defined mission, the health and vitality of the funding source, and any established traditions, preferences, or brand loyalties already in place. U.S. law enforcement agencies tend to buy their new helicopters from Bell Helicopter Textron, McDonnell Douglas, and American Eurocopter. Other ships in service include ex-military or government surplus (like the Huey), and a smattering of offerings from Enstrom, Robinson, Sikorsky, and Schweizer. The base price for a new helicopter is governed by the type of engine (piston or turbine), number of

engines (single or twin), cabin capacity, gross weight capability, speed, and range. These elements also either define or limit the mission.

Like motorcycles and hot rods, helicopters are categorized by engine type and size. There are four broad categories of helicopter powerplants sold in the law enforcement market: piston, single turbine, light twin turbine, and medium twin turbine. On the low end of the powerplant range is the piston engine, best exemplified by the Robinson 22. Although its capabilities may be limited, it fills a narrow but important niche as a law enforcement tool. The R-22 is a weight-critical two-seater with little tolerance for anything too heavy, including its pilot and observer, thus limiting the size of a spotlight, and eliminating a forward-looking infrared (FLIR) imager as an option. The R-22 is powered by a 160-horsepower Textron Lycoming 0-320-B2C piston engine. Acquisition and maintenance costs are very low.

The next category is the single-turbine engine. About 95 percent of helicopters used for law enforcement are single turbines. These include the Bell JetRanger, the McDonnell Douglas 500 Series, the American Eurocopter AS350, and the Bell LongRanger. These are typically used for patrol and have sufficient horsepower to handle the crew, specialized law enforcement equipment (FLIR, spotlight, and so on), and an additional passenger or two if necessary.

The McDonnell Douglas 500 Series has long been the workhorse of many police departments across the country. The MD 500E is classified as a high-performance light helicopter. Its standard engine is a 420-shaft-horsepower Allison 250-C20B. The 500E offers an optional engine with 450 shaft

horsepower. The MD 500F looks like the E model but offers a larger standard engine. The Allison 250-C30 turbine develops 650 shaft horsepower and its main rotor is one foot (30.5cm) greater in diameter than the E model. These two features allow the 500F to operate in hot climates and at higher altitudes than the 500E.

The most current rotor technology available for patrol today is the McDonnell Douglas 520N, or NOTAR (for "no tail rotor"). It's quieter and more powerful than its classic older brother, the MD 500E. The NOTAR replaces the conventional tail-rotor design with a fan-driven system located in the tail boom. This system produces a current of air that counteracts the torque of the main rotor. The design of the tail boom also contributes significantly to torque counteraction.

The MD 520N's fuselage looks very similar to that of the MD 500E, except the tail boom is much larger in diameter and

The California Highway Patrol uses the Bell LongRanger to patrol California's thousands of highway miles. Mounted under the nose is a large searchlight. The angular extensions above and below the cockpit are wire cutters, used in an emergency if the pilot accidentally flys into a telephone or power line.

The McDonnell Douglas 520N NOTAR has quickly become a favorite of many police departments. NOTAR technology counteracts torque by using the air forced down over the tail boom by the main rotor in conjunction with air forced through openings in the tail boom. When certified by the FAA, the 520N was the quietest helicopter ever evaluated. This one is in the service of the Los Angeles County's Sheriff's department.

This Los Angeles County MD500 helicopter has just landed in the parking lot of an industrial park. The pilot, in the right seat, has opened his door to let some cool air in, as the observer removes gear from the back seat.

there is no tail rotor. The 520N is powered by an Allison 250-C20R turbo shaft engine producing a maximum of 475 shaft horsepower. The 520N's five-bladed main rotor is twenty-six feet, five inches (8.1m) in diameter. Cruising speed for the 520N is 144 miles per hour (231.7kph).

Within the 520N's tail boom, at the rear of the fuselage, is a constant-speed variable-pitch fan with thirteen thermoplastic blades. This fan draws air in from the top of the fuselage, just rear of the rotor hub. The air is pushed the length of the composite tail boom and exits through slots in the right side and through the direct jet thruster, near the end of the tail boom. The direct jet thruster supplies only part of the thrust required to counteract torque. The main component of torque counteraction is provided by the innovative design of the tail boom, which redirects the main rotor's downwash around the tail boom to the left, creating lateral lift. The foot pedals control yaw by varying the pitch of the fan, resulting in more or

less air being forced out of the direct jet thruster. The vertical stabilizer located on the left side of the tail is also controlled by foot pedals.

The NOTAR is an exceptionally quiet helicopter. This is a big benefit for law enforcement. Citizens are happy that the police helicopter patrolling above will not interrupt an over-the-fence conversation between neighbors. This translates into fewer citizen complaints of noise. Police like it because it offers them a certain degree of stealth in performing their enforcement duties.

The newest NOTAR helicopter from McDonnell Douglas is the MD 600N. It features a lengthened fuselage with comfortable seating for up to eight passengers, as well as a more powerful 808-shaft-horsepower Allison 250-C47 turbine engine. This stretched-out version of the MD 520N has greater lifting capacity, is capable of increased speed, and sports several new safety features.

The nimble McDonnell Douglas 500 is favored by many police department air units. Attached to the underside of the fuselage on both of these helicopters is a small searchlight. Weight is a factor on this smaller helicopter, precluding the use of a FLIR unit.

The Bell JetRanger, manufactured by Bell Helicopter Textron, is one of the most recognizable helicopters in the United States. Since the first one was delivered in 1971, more than 7,000 have been built. The Bell JetRanger was the first helicopter to fly around the world. The JetRanger is powered by an Allison 250-C20J engine producing 420 shaft horsepower. Its two-bladed all-metal rotor is thirty-three feet, four inches (10.2m) in diameter.

Bell's JetRanger and LongRanger look very much alike. The LongRanger is about two feet (61cm) longer in the cabin area and can be identified by its three side windows. This additional length provides space for two more passengers than the five-passenger JetRanger. The cabin in both designs is a semi-monocoque construction of bonded aluminum honeycomb. The LongRanger is powered by an Allison 250-C30P engine that produces 650 horsepower. Like the JetRanger's, the LongRanger's main rotor is all metal but larger, measuring a full thirty-seven feet (11.3m) in diameter.

The twin-turbine configurations (which in general are larger vehicles) are the next category of law enforcement helicopter. This market is relatively small for police use, reserved generally for those units with an EMS mission, and includes the American Eurocopter AS355 TwinStar and B0105 Series or the Bell 206LT TwinRanger.

During a training exercise, three members of the Phoenix, Arizona, Police Department's SWAT unit catch a ride on one of the department's MD 520N NOTAR helicopters.

With its injured passenger safely aboard, this Bell LongRanger is lifting off, en route to a trauma center. Landing and taking off from city streets presents a unique set of challenges for the helicopter pilot. A city street is typically lined with trees, power lines, and vehicles, all hazards to a helicopter.

SPECIAL DEVICES FOR COMMUNICATION, NAVIGATION, AND SURVEILLANCE

Law enforcement helicopters used for routine patrol have varying degrees of sophistication in these three areas: communication, navigation, and surveillance. FAA regulations mandate minimum levels of communication and navigation for safe flight operations into and out of controlled airspace. Some law enforcement air units may use a variety of radio frequencies, from the standard VHF aircraft radio to 800MHz trunked lines, the most sophisticated and efficient way to use available radio frequencies for communication among several agencies. Some systems allow the pilot and observer to talk on separate (primary and secondary) frequencies.

Some units are lucky enough to have a GPS navigation and mapping system. This allows them to create beat numbers denoting sectors of the city. Beat numbers display on a moving map, indicating their locations. Conversely, selecting a beat number will give a correct course heading, nautical miles, and time to the next call. The GPS system can be programmed to indicate when the helicopter is entering a dedicated flight path for other aircraft—a must for positive-controlled airspace, where commercial and general aviation and military aircraft all compete for the sky.

One of the most sought-after search, surveillance, and evidence-gathering tools is FLIR, which picks up radiated heat from objects on the ground, then amplifies and converts this information into a video image displayed on a monitor in the cockpit. FLIR is most useful and effective at night. The technology is used most often to locate a suspect attempting to evade or hide from police officers. FLIR can reveal inanimate objects, too, like the heated brake drums or engine compartment of a recently driven vehicle, otherwise invisible in a dark, remote location. (One police air unit sent its officers into a field at night to check out an image on the FLIR, which appeared to be the hot spot generated by a person hiding. Immediately after the officers arrived at the location, they were briskly walking away waving their arms. When the air unit radioed the ground officers to ask why they walked away from what appeared to be a suspect, the ground officer's agitated reply was "Beehive!")

A valuable high-tech item available to air units is a FLIR system that functions not only as a standard FLIR imager but as a color video camera with a high-resolution picture. A Super VHS recorder is installed in the rear of the helicopter to capture the action as seen through the FLIR camera. A videotape created with this technology is a valuable and reliable piece of evidence when a suspect is brought to trial.

For night patrol, many departments use the Nightsun SX 16, a 1,600-watt searchlight with thirty million candlepower. Smaller lights are available for weight-critical helicopters. The light can be mounted on the nose, rear, or side of the aircraft. The direction and beam width of the light are controlled from the cockpit. As a law enforcement tool, the light beam

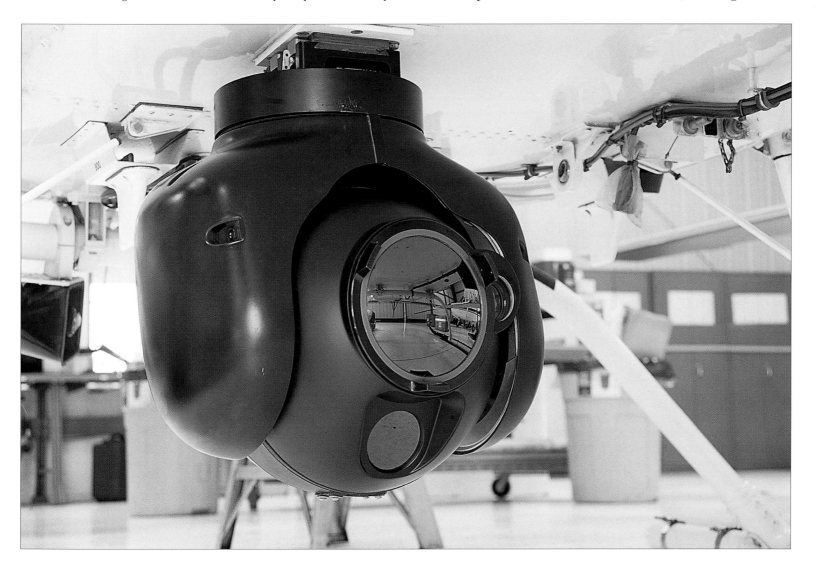

Slung under the belly of this police helicopter is a FLIR. The FLIR senses the heat given off by objects below and displays the images on a screen in the cockpit. It is one of the most valuable tools for airborne police units.

announces the arrival of yet another set of officers to the scene, contains the area by virtue of its presence, and searches areas otherwise inaccessible or unsafe for ground officers. When a fleeing suspect gets hit with a spotlight, it's like throwing a net over him. There's just no way to lose the light. Directed by the observing officer hovering above, ground units simply close in.

A public address/siren system is necessary for a tactical helicopter. The siren's "yelp and wail" gets the attention of a crowd or group of bystanders below. Then using the P.A. system, the crew can instruct people to move away from a dangerous situation or simply direct them as needed.

Another handy tool is a pair of gyrostabilized binoculars. Counteracting the vibration and movement in a helicopter, this device enables the observer to look for a suspect, read a license plate number, or call out a street address to ground units.

The H-34 Choctaw was used by the U.S. military in the early 1960s, before the introduction of the Huey. It was originally powered by a large radial engine located in the nose. This Los Angeles County Sheriff's Department chopper has been converted to a lighter and more powerful gas turbine engine. The two large nostrils on the front of the cowling provide air to the new powerplant. The winch above the cargo door confirms that this helicopter is used for rescues in the rugged mountainous areas of Southern California. The crew chief is about to pull the chocks from the main gear in preparation for takeoff.

Converted Hueys make outstanding rescue helicopters. Airframes and parts are plentiful and relatively inexpensive.

ROTOR TALES—TRUE STORIES FROM THE SKY

A Police Helicopter's Technology Locates a Hidden Suspect

It was a late-night shift, around midnight, when my pilot, Chuck Belletti, and I received a radio call reporting a burglary in progress. It was at a downtown warehouse and we were the first ones on the scene. We orbited the warehouse at about 400 feet [122m], holding the perimeter and watching for anything out of the ordinary. It was a two-story metal corrugated warehouse and everything seemed normal. The ground units arrived and did a quick search. They were waiting for a canine unit to arrive and start their search. The whole process was taking a lot of time, probably a good twenty minutes to twenty-five minutes, waiting for all the officers to get there to do the search. In the meantime, we continued orbiting, maintaining the perimeter, and watching for anybody running from the building.

Watching with the helicopter's infrared, I noticed that a part of the metal building started to glow. This hot spot was on the west side of the building, at the second story level. It was in the shape of a triangle, about a foot and a half [46cm] tall by a foot [30.5cm]) wide. Each time we circled, the hot spot got brighter and brighter. From the air, I watched the officers disappear into the building for their search and then come out. I thought the only thing that could cause the metal to heat up like that was possibly a generator that had kicked on and started to heat up the wall of the building. When the officers went inside to search the building, I asked them to check the second story where I saw the hot spot. From the air I could also see a piece of metal that had been peeled away from the wall, probably about three to four yards [2.7m–3.7m] away from the hot spot. We were also keeping an eye on that opening to make sure nobody could squeeze out. I looked at it with the binoculars and could see graffiti spray-painted on the side of the metal. I picked out a particular letter of that graffiti so I could communicate an exact location to the officer on the ground who was holding the perimeter. He was looking at that hole to make sure nobody came through. From that point on the wall, I could relate to him the exact location of the hot spot. Between the two of us, we could communicate that precise position to the officers inside the building. The officers went in and did a cursory look through that area. They said that there was just a bunch of trash piled up inside that section of the building, and then they left. I asked if there was a generator or something in there that caused that area of the metal building to heat up. The heat signature I was seeing was very consistent with a suspect hiding in there. I figured he was trying to get back to his little hole in the wall to get out.

The officer on the ground and I were very insistent on searching again. The officers went back inside with canines and searched that specific area once more. This time they pulled out all the trash, Styrofoam, and junk that had been piled up. That's where the guy was hiding! He had tucked himself back there in the corner of the building against the wall and had pulled all the trash bags and Styrofoam over himself—he'd been hiding in there the whole time. His body heat was heating up the metal wall he was leaning against and that's what I saw on the FLIR.

—Officer-Pilot Teresa Clark
San Diego Police Department
Air Support Unit

Officer Teresa Clark has been a member of the San Diego Police Department for eleven years. She has been flying helicopters for four years and is a certified flight instructor for both helicopters and fixed-wing aircraft.

BIBLIOGRAPHY

Chant, Christoper. *Bell UH-1 Super Profile*. London: Winchmore Publishing
Services Ltd., 1985.

Cook, John L. *Dust Off*. New York: Bantam Books, 1988.

Fay, John. *The Helicopter: History, Piloting & How it Flies*. Great Britain:
David & Charles Publishers, 1987.

Jackson, Paul. *Jane's All the World's Aircraft 1996–97*. Surrey, England: Jane's
Information Group Ltd., 1996.

Lightbody, Andy, and Joe Poyer. *The Illustrated History of Helicopters*.
Lincolnwood, Illinois: Publications International, Ltd., 1990.

Marvicsin, Dennis J., and Jerold A. Greenfield *Maverick: The Personal War of
a Vietnam Cobra Pilot*. New York: G.P. Putnam's Sons, 1990.

Mondey, David. *The International Encyclopedia of Aviation*. New York:
Crown Publishers, Inc., 1977.

Rendall, David. *Jane's Aircraft Recognition Guide*. Glasgow, Scotland:
HarperCollins Publishers, 1996.

Young, Warren R. *The Helicopters*. Time-Life Books, 1987.

A versatile eight-seat MD 600N single-turbine NOTAR chopper floats gracefully over water in tourist service in Mesa, Arizona.